LEGENDS OF THE NEW ENGLAND COAST

★ LEGENDS OF ★
THE NEW ENGLAND COAST

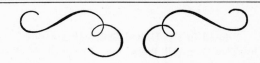

BY

EDWARD ROWE SNOW

ILLUSTRATED

DODD, MEAD & COMPANY

NEW YORK, 1957

TO

ANNA-MYRLE

MY WIFE

AND

MOTHER OF OUR DAUGHTER

DOROTHY CAROLINE

THIS VOLUME IS

AFFECTIONATELY DEDICATED

INTRODUCTION

IN THE LIFE of every book there comes a time when the writer realizes that most of the important work has been finished and that he may relax just a little in order to explain to those of the anxious public as best he can what is in the volume. That point in this book, *Legends of the New England Coast,* has on this day of October 4, 1957, been reached.

There is a certain joy of heart in writing these few words of introduction or explanation after the exacting but strangely pleasant task of writing is over.

In this book there are twenty-nine chapters concerning unusual legends and stories on and off the vast New England shore line.

The case of the *Andrea Doria,* rapidly becoming one of the great New England legends, begins the volume. The tale of the million dollar gamble with the *Etrusco* is still another unusual account of man and the sea. The mermaid chapter should interest those of you who hitherto have specialized in discussions about whether or not sea serpents really exist.

A visit is made to Cape Cod for the Legend of Scargo Lake, while the tale of White Horse Beach may intrigue those who find unusual fascination in love stories. Maine's Phantom Ship and the strange ghost seen on Grand Manan may attract those who delve into the supernatural, while the sad fate of Anthony Collamore should interest all of you.

Among the many legends which I have enjoyed ferreting out are included the Mantle of Death, the Sparrow-Hawk, the Galleon of 1616, Ocean Born Mary, and Lithobolia.

Every New England state except Vermont has its important part in this volume, with Maine, New Hampshire and Massachusetts providing the major share of the legends. The Rhode Island accounts feature the burning of the *Gaspée*, many of the details of which have been obscure in the mind of the average resident of Rhode Island. The delightfully weird life of Newport's Tom Tew, the pirate who apparently commuted between his wife and home in Newport and his wife and home on an island off the African coast, is included in this book.

Legends concerning that part which women have played in New England coastal history include the story of the real Pocahontas; the unwed maid of Marblehead, Agnes Surriage; Goody Cole, the witch of Hampton, New Hampshire; Ocean Born Mary; and Marramette, the Indian maiden of the Neponset River.

Incidentally, I am especially grateful to Mr. Robb Sagendorph of the *Yankee* Magazine for his generosity in allowing me to use sections of the material I wrote which appeared in his publication, including the Mermaid story as well as accounts of the *Etrusco* and the *Sparrow-Hawk*. John R. Herbert, editor of the Quincy *Patriot-Ledger*, has been more than kind in his furthering of my nautical writing efforts.

My wife, Anna-Myrle, did wonderful work in seeing that the various dead-lines were reached on time, and I am forever grateful for her help.

The following paragraph is composed entirely of a list of those who have helped me in one way or another in gathering material for this book. Others are mentioned directly in the text.

Donald B. Akerstrom, Jr., TM 3 (SS), Alton Hall Blackington, Mary E. Brown, G. W. Browne, Frank P. Bruno, Blanche Cummings, Patricia Donlin, Ella W. Eldridge, L. Whitney Elkins, Richard Fallona, G. T. Ferris, Jacquelyn Findlay, Lillian E. Finnie, Rev. Daniel A. Flynn, Olivo Frugoli, Margaret Hackett, Lyttle Hall, Marie Hansen, Arthur M. Harrington, Bradford M. Hill, Syd Jarman, Carleton Leslie Joyce, Margaret D. Joyce, Allen T. Klots, Jr., Commander R. Gordon H. Maclane, Virginia Marini, Ruth R. Merrill, Hans Neuhauser, Beulah Sylvester Oxton, Walter Paul, Dorothy Perkins, Ronald Poole, Charles Randall, Lawrence Rideout, Stephen D. Riley, Anna D. Rowe, Phyllis J. Scorza, Court Simmons, Isaac M. Small, Lillian May Small, Alice Rowe Snow, Dorothy Caroline Snow, John R. Spears, Journalist Eugene R. Toner, Charles Wood, and William G. Vinal.

The Boston Public Library, the Bostonian Society, the Massachusetts Historical Society, the Harvard College Library, the Boston Athenaeum, the Peabody Museum, the Essex Institute, and the American Antiquarian Society have generously allowed me the use of material in their vaults.

Incidentally, I am particularly pleased with the 1833 painting in full color by Robert Salmon which appears on the dust jacket of the book. I have always shared the enthusiasm art expert Charles D. Childs of Boston shows for beautiful marines which Salmon created over a century ago. The mystery of Salmon's life may never be solved, but his paintings remain with us, a joy for everyone. In my *Cruising the Massachusetts Coast* there is a black and white reproduction of Salmon's painting of Governor's Island.

Quite often people have a mistaken impression of what a legend is. In order that no one reading this book starts off with a misconception concerning that important word LEGEND, let us examine what the authorities say about it.

The various dictionaries tell us that a legend may be "a story of life, or a collection of such stories." Hence, it is "a narrative, or a history." A legend is also "any story coming down from the past, one popularly taken as historical, although not verifiable." In this book are included legends under all of the above classifications.

Most of the work for this book was done in my study, where I am seated at the present moment. The room faces northeast toward the new 1898 mouth of the famed North River. My study windows also look out over the marshes of Marshfield.

Whenever I become too exhausted in research and writing I step out of the back door, walk down the old ox-cart trail which our daughter Dorothy Caroline affectionately calls "down path" and enter a world which could almost be called a "forest primeval."

My canoe is moored to a stake, reached by a walk down the trail and then off the trail to the marsh. Dropping the canoe into the tiny tidal rivulet nearby, I am soon ocean-bound out of the North River.

After my trip from trail to rivulet to river to ocean, I return to the study, refreshed and ready for the next problem or chapter. The present book was written and finished with many such refreshing interludes, and it is my hope that its pages may prove of interest to you. Let me hear from you about it.

EDWARD ROWE SNOW

Marshfield, Massachusetts

CONTENTS

ILLUSTRATIONS

LEGENDS OF THE NEW ENGLAND COAST

ANDREA DORIA

As DARKNESS FELL on a fog-enshrouded sea off Nantucket Island on the night of July 25, 1956, in an area known as the Times Square of the North Atlantic, the 697-foot Italian luxury liner *Andrea Doria* * moved rapidly through the glasslike surface of the ocean. Although there had been an offshore fog for three days, the giant liner was still expected to arrive on schedule in New York early the next morning. She had left Genoa eight days before, stopping at various Mediterranean ports before sailing out through the Strait of Gibraltar into the open sea. Aboard the pride of the Italian Line were more than seventeen hundred people.

The last glimmer of New England daylight disappeared, and the early evening hours passed. Flushed with the excitement of approaching their homeland again, returning American tourists mingled with immigrants plan-

---

* Named for a sixteenth-century prince who defended Genoa from her enemies.

ning to settle in the New World. Important personalities of society and the business world celebrated with political leaders, screen stars, physicians and newsmen.

Some miles to the eastward, similar gatherings were taking place aboard another vessel, outward-bound. Passengers of the 12,165-ton Swedish-American liner *Stockholm,* which had left New York for Europe at 11:30 that same morning, were filled with anticipation for the coming journey. Their first night out on the ocean, they were trying their sea legs. Back in New York Harbor that morning the smaller, 510-foot *Stockholm* had waited briefly as the mammoth, 44,500-ton transatlantic veteran, the *Ile de France* took the lead down the bay. After sailing out through the Narrows, the two craft had soon disappeared over the horizon.

By eleven o'clock that fateful night the *Andrea Doria,* *Stockholm* and *Ile de France* were in the general vicinity of the Nantucket Lightship. In relatively easy range were the *Pvt. W. H. Thomas,* the *Cape Ann* and the destroyer escort *Edward H. Allen.*

There were many activities in progress aboard the *Andrea Doria.* In one of the four spacious theaters a moving picture, *Foxfire,* was being shown. In the luxurious Belvedere Lounge on the boat deck an orchestra entertained dancers as they glided over the waxed floor. Down below, tiers of baggage already crowded the passageways, ready for the next day's exodus, while throughout the ship scores of weary voyagers were sound asleep in their cabins.

For three full days foggy weather had covered the entire sea area from Newfoundland down to Martha's Vineyard, and mariners were unhappily attempting to make up for lost time. Nearer and nearer to each other came the

Stockholm and the *Andrea Doria.* Then suddenly card players aboard the Italian vessel stared in horror at the chilling sight of another vessel's lights surging toward them out of the mist. A moment later, with a terrifying crash of snapping girders and bulkheads, the *Stockholm* plowed into the starboard side of the *Doria* immediately abaft her flying bridge.

The two vessels held together in their unnatural union for a split second and then seemed to leap apart in a dazzling shower of sparks. The *Stockholm's* sharp bow, which had been rebuilt for use as an icebreaker, had punched a fatal hole into the Italian liner. The jagged gash torn into her side was forty feet wide and thirty feet deep, extending more than fifty feet above and at least fifteen feet below the water line.

All over the *Doria* the collision caught the passengers and crew, and tossed them about mercilessly. The shock dropped the dancers to the deck and ripped the card tables away from the players. In the bar patrons were sprinkled with cascades of flying glass, and those in the auditorium watching the moving pictures were jumbled together in startled heaps. Hundreds of passengers, asleep in beds and bunks, were hurled about in their cabins, while far below in the bowels of the ship, crew members, recovering from the crash, soberly prepared for whatever might lie ahead. Out in the corridors smoke and dust from the collision began to settle over the masses of baggage, now flung about in hopeless confusion.

Captain Piero Calamai, master of the *Andrea Doria,* quickly took command of the situation. Discovering the seriousness of the wound which the *Stockholm* had dealt his beloved craft, the captain ordered his radio operator to send out an appeal for help.

At approximately 11:22 P.M. Eastern Daylight Time, a distress message flashed through the air, excerpts from which follow: SOS . . . COLLISION . . . SEND IMMEDIATE ASSISTANCE.

The latitude given at the time was 40° 30′ N, and the longitude was 60° 53′ west.

The stricken Italian craft, with tons of water pouring into her gaping wound every second, began to list over on her starboard side almost at once. Soon the cant of the deck approximated 25 degrees. A short time later it was 35 degrees!

Within the next two hours eight crowded lifeboats were released. The officers now appealed by radio for additional boats, for with the port deck at a precarious angle of 45 degrees, none could be launched from that side. Finally the angle of the deck became so pronounced that the water from the *Doria's* swimming pools came flowing across the deck to stream into the sea.

While the mighty liner was gradually submerging beneath them, little groups of frightened passengers, uncertain of the seriousness of their plight, gathered together and clung to one another in various parts of the giant ship. Some told jokes, while others took turns praying.

Several craft which had been in the vicinity were now arriving to lend assistance to the stricken vessel with lifeboats and motor tenders. Captain Gunnar Nordenson of the *Stockholm*, having examined his own ship and found her seaworthy, sent across lifeboats for rescue work.

The fog now lifted to reveal for the first time the beautiful 793-foot French liner *Ile de France* sliding into full view. Every light on the ship proved a comforting sight to the frightened people still aboard the *Andrea Doria*

which even at this time appeared to some to be capable
of staying afloat indefinitely.

By this time the *Doria* had actually released ten of her
own lifeboats and the *Ile de France* began taking off the
survivors at once. The *Pvt. W. H. Thomas* and the *Cape
Ann* were soon removing their share of the passengers.
Later the *Edward H. Allen* joined in the rescue work.

These efforts continued through the night. The tanker
Hopkins, sailing from Revere, Massachusetts, picked up
one man, Robert L. Hudson, whom they found hanging
to the debarkation net. The *Stockholm* took off 570 people and the *Cape Ann,* 129. The *Thomas* picked up 165
survivors, the *Ile de France,* 758, and the destroyer escort
Edward H. Allen, 77, from the sinking Italian liner.

At 8:15 on the morning of July 26 the Coast Guard cut-
ter *Evergreen* took over command of the situation from
the *Thomas* which, as a government vessel, had assumed
nominal control of the operation. Other Coast Guard craft
soon arrived on the scene, the *Yakutat,* the *Campbell,* the
Hornbeam and the *Owasco.*

Captain Calamai and the last Italian crewman left the
Doria by 7:00, giving up the unequal struggle between
man and sea, for they realized that the water would continue to pour into the mortal gash made by the *Stockholm* until the ship went down.

Flying above the stricken ship, one could notice the
change in her position by 8:25 that morning. The sea was
then lapping around the *Doria's* starboard rail, and the
port propeller could easily be seen above the surface.

With the coming of dawn helicopters and airplanes
were literally swarming around the disaster area. At ten
o'clock Bob Cadigan of the Nantucket Flying Service
passed low over the scene and found the decks of the

Doria awash. Shortly afterward six lifeboats ripped loose and came to the surface. Giant geysers spurted forth from the amidships section, rising seventy and eighty feet. The great vessel was now down by the bow. At the last moment her stern appeared to rise slightly above the surface of the sea, as if making a final effort to stay afloat. The port propeller broke water along its entire shaft, and there was foam ten feet deep by her stern. Then, at 10:09 A.M., she simply slid over and went under, leaving lifeboats and other wreckage swirling around on the surface and masses of green, bubbling water everywhere.

The *Andrea Doria* had scarcely disappeared before another plane, piloted by my good friend Ralph Hynes of the Wiggins Airport in Norwood passed over the spot. Hynes later said of this experience:

"I had Captain Carlo Fava, the New England representative of the Italian Line, aboard with me, but when we got over the scene, there was nothing but wreckage left. The *Andrea Doria* was gone."

Hundreds of individual episodes of heroism and tragedy were enacted that fateful night, only a few examples of which I mention here. Mr. and Mrs. Tullio di Sandro were aboard the Italian ship with their four-and-a-half-year-old daughter, Norma. When a lifeboat from the *Stockholm* maneuvered immediately below the dangerously canted liner, Mr. di Sandro became panic-stricken for fear that the *Doria* was about to sink. Shouting down to a member of the lifeboat crew, he dropped his little daughter over the side to the sailor. To everyone's horror, her body turned in the air and she struck her head on the lifeboat. Mr. and Mrs. di Sandro were unable to follow their daughter into the lifeboat, and the unconscious girl was taken to the *Stockholm* and later flown ashore in a helicopter without their knowledge.

Landing at Nantucket Airport, Norma was first examined by physicians of the Cottage Hospital. Her condition was so serious that she was rushed by Coast Guard airplane to Boston's Logan Airport and from there was hurried to the Brighton Marine Hospital nearby.

Meanwhile her desperate parents were taken aboard the *Ile de France* and brought to New York. There the frantic couple learned that a young child with a ram's horn charm bracelet which they knew Norma was wearing, was a patient at the Marine Hospital. They arrived in Brighton at 3:30 the next morning, but little Norma never regained consciousness and died eighteen hours later.

When the two vessels came together actress Ruth Roman rushed into her stateroom to tell her sleeping three-year-old son to get ready for "a picnic," but she became separated from her child during the confusion. After many agonizing hours, they had a joyous reunion at a New York pier.

Colonel Walter Carlin of Brooklyn, prominent in political circles, discovered in shocked surprise on returning from the washroom after the collision that not only had his wife vanished but their cabin had disappeared as well! Mrs. Carlin had been instantly killed in the crash.

The most unbelievable story of the entire disaster was that of fourteen-year-old Linda Morgan, who with her family shared two staterooms on the Italian liner. The *Stockholm* smashed into the very rooms in which they were sleeping. Missing after the collision, Linda was officially listed as dead. What actually happened was no less than a miracle.

Aboard the Swedish liner *Stockholm* was thirty-six-year-old crewman Bernabe Garcia, who had gone to bed at 9:45 that night. When the crash came, he had just dozed off from his reading of Strindberg's *Röda Rummet*. Stumbling to his feet, he felt the strong pull of reversing engines as he made his way toward a Babel of voices forward.

In the darkness he noticed how the bow of the *Stockholm* had been crumpled by the collision. Then he heard a voice and began to walk toward the sound, a confused cry that ended in a sob. Ahead of him, there was a mass of debris, but he fought his way through it. Finally he discovered the head and shoulders of a girl buried to her waist in wreckage.

Garcia cried out for others to aid him. When no one came he attempted to pull the child from the rubble by himself without injuring her. Then, suddenly the girl spoke.

"*¿Donde esta Mama?*"

Instinctively the Spaniard answered her. "Was your mama here? I am a native of Cádiz."

"She was here with me. What has happened?"

Garcia then explained to the girl that at the moment of the collision in some unexplainable way she had been scooped up by the *Stockholm's* bow from her bed on the *Andrea Doria*, and that she was caught in the debris on the Swedish vessel. He managed to work the Morgan girl free within a few minutes. Carrying her aft, he handed Linda over to a Danish gentleman, who took her to the ship's sick bay. Meanwhile, Garcia scrambled back to the bow wreckage in a futile attempt to discover Linda's mother.

Suddenly he sighted the remains of a blonde woman,

but a moment later, before he could reach it, the body
slipped off into the sea with several broken fragments of
the bow. Without question the woman had been killed
instantly at the moment of collision, but it turned out that
she was not Linda's mother. Linda's stepfather, Camille
M. Cianfarra, Madrid correspondent of *The New York
Times*, and Linda's stepsister Joan, were killed, but the
mother, although injured, was still alive aboard the *Doria*.

Another terrifying incident involved Dr. Thure C. Peterson, a chiropractor of Upper Montclair, New Jersey,
and his wife, Martha. The *Stockholm's* bow plowed right
through their cabin, pinning Mrs. Peterson by the spine
and legs to the broken wreckage of the deck, after which
the ship backed away again.

Struggling through the wreckage, Dr. Peterson discovered not only his wife but also Mrs. Cianfarra, both of
whom were cruelly pinioned by the twisted steel girders.
After attempting in vain to rescue his own wife with the
aid of a crewman named Gino, Peterson lifted Mrs. Cianfarra free from the debris.

As the initial glow of the false dawn came, Dr. Peterson
noticed for the first time that he was working on a tiny
triangle of twisted metal, which was suspended high
above the water like an island in the sky. At any minute
the entire mass might slip off into the sea.

The moment that he had freed Mrs. Cianfarra, Dr. Peterson again attempted to cut away the steel which had
caught his wife, but was still unable to do so. Searching
for something which might push the wreckage free from
his wife's body, Peterson found a jack. Together he and
Gino wedged the heavy tool under the wreckage and the
mass began to move. But at that very moment Mrs. Peterson spoke to her husband.

"I'm going," she said quietly. A moment later she was dead.

Few readers realize that there was another collision besides that of the *Andrea Doria* and the *Stockholm* which occurred under identical circumstances in the same sea lanes and in the same fog less than two days before, when the freighter *Fairisle* and the Panamanian tanker *San José II* collided. The twelve members of the injured *Fairisle* were removed by the Coast Guard. Efforts to bring her into port failed when the craft settled on the bottom in shallow water at Gravesend Bay. She was later raised, repaired and put back in service.

For more than a century members of the human race have been killed in similar disasters because of the sacrifice of safety for speed in fog. One hundred and six years before, on June 28, 1850, the American "Clipper of the Seas," *Arctic*, was launched in New York, and was at once accepted as a challenge to England's dominance of the Atlantic speed records.

On September 20, 1854, the *Arctic* sailed from Liverpool for New York. Shortly after noon on September 27, however, a terrified lookout screamed a warning that another craft was approaching in the fog. Before anyone could act to change course sufficiently, the small French screw steamer *Vesta* hit the guards of the *Arctic*, fatally wounding her as the *Stockholm* was to injure the *Andrea Doria* one hundred and two years later.

In the undisciplined confusion which followed, only eighty-three persons survived, and the *Arctic* went down with three hundred and five perishing in the sea! The *Vesta* limped through the ocean to Saint John's, Newfoundland, reaching there on September 30.

And so it has gone year after year. Indeed the terrible

toll of ships out on the ocean began soon after the earliest navigator "had the unheard of audacity" to venture out on the bosom of the sea. Almost every decade since has brought its tale of suffering and woe. Of course, nature herself with storms, icebergs and fog has contributed tremendously to the disaster list during the passing centuries, but beginning with the *Arctic* in the year 1854, I blame man for most of the heartrending marine tragedies which have occurred.*

The steamer *Titanic,* rated at the time just as unsinkable as the *Andrea Doria,* had been constructed with a new system of watertight compartments that the builders claimed could be closed from the bridge of the 882-foot White Star super liner within a few seconds. Even though her entire bow or stern might be stove in, the designers were certain that the ship still could not sink. The massive craft had eleven steel decks which could be made into fifteen watertight bulkheads.

The *Titanic,* then the world's largest vessel, left on her maiden voyage from England on April 10, 1912. All went well the first few days. Then the weather grew chillier for the vessel was approaching the region of ice floes. At 8:55 on the night of April 14, 1912, Captain E. J. Smith came on the bridge to announce that he had just received

* Examples include the loss of the *Lyonnais* in 1856, the *Pomona* in 1859, the *Sultana* in 1865, the *City of Boston* in 1872, the *Cambria* in 1883, the *Portland* in 1898, the *General Slocum* in 1904, the *Larchmont* in 1907, the *Titanic* in 1912, the *Empress of Ireland* in 1914, the *Eastland* in 1915, the *Egypt* in 1922, the *Morro Castle* in 1934, the *Noronic* in 1949, and the *Hobson* in 1952. Conditions in the vicinity of the Nantucket Lightship eventually caused the government to move her location. On January 23, 1909, the White Star Liner *Republic* was rammed by the Italian Liner *Florida* in a dense fog. The lightship herself was cut in two by the *Olympic* on May 16, 1934. On October 2, 1954, the *Maasdam* and the *Tofero* collided. The lightship was moved 15 miles out to sea in March, 1953, and again moved on January 1, 1956.

wireless reports from the *Olympic* and the *Baltic*, then sailing in the same general area, that there were ice fields and icebergs ahead. Half an hour later Captain Smith went below.

Shortly after 10:00, in the crow's nest high above the deck of the *Titanic*, Seaman Frederick Fleet gave an incredulous shout. He had just sighted a gigantic iceberg directly in the path of the liner. Notifying the bridge at once, the frightened sailor was gratified when he felt a pronounced but sickening swerve of the *Titanic* to port, out of the way of the visible part of the berg. Realizing that an iceberg's bulk is nine tenths submerged, Fleet prayed that the giant craft would clear it under water.

Unfortunately a steel-like spur of the giant berg extended far out in the course of the oncoming ship. The vessel's swerve was too late and the spur acted as a huge can opener, ripping a long gash in the "unsinkable" liner. It was her death blow, for soon began a list to port which continued until she finally disappeared beneath the surface.*

When the *Andrea Doria* was completed in 1951, it was claimed by her builders, as the builders of the *Titanic* had claimed two generations before, that the hull had been specially constructed not only to prevent her from ever sinking but to give her more stability in case of collision. The *Doria's* hull was subdivided into eleven watertight compartments which extended the entire length of the ship. Bulkheads parallel with her engine rooms were also designed to lessen the effect of a crash at sea. Her builders were certain that she was unsinkable.

If the *Andrea Doria* was built according to the stand-

---

* Of the 2340 who had sailed aboard her, 1503 drowned when the *Titanic* foundered in the icy seas.

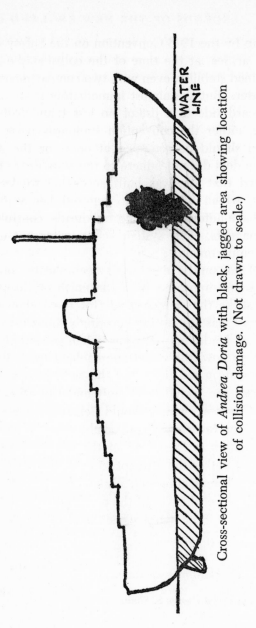

WATER LINE

Cross-sectional view of *Andrea Doria* with black, jagged area showing location of collision damage. (Not drawn to scale.)

ards set up by the 1948 Convention on the Safety of Human Life at Sea, at the time of the collision she should have retained stability, even with two compartments open to the water. But she almost immediately went over on her starboard side to a list of no less than 25 degrees! Therefore, either the convention standards were inadequate and should be scrapped at once, or the *Andrea Doria's* builders did not adhere to the standards. It is to be doubted that she was built according to American standards, which would have required her watertight doors to have automatic sealing bulkheads, controlled by electric magnets. This system keeps water out of connecting compartments.

Right of way on the high seas is a complicated problem. The *Stockholm* appeared from the north of the *Andrea Doria* to strike the starboard side of the Italian vessel. Neither craft was attempting knowingly to cross the path of the other. Under maritime law, when one ship is crossing another's bow, the vessel approaching from the starboard, showing a red light, has the right of way. Thus she becomes the "privileged" craft and the other is the "burdened" vessel, which should "change course, slow down, stop or reverse, or any combination of these actions," necessary to "keep out of the way." If the burdened vessel makes the attempt to cross the other's bow and thereby brings about a collision, she is at fault for not keeping out of the way of the privileged vessel.*

However it will be extremely difficult to decide to the satisfaction of all concerned which, if either, was the privileged craft on the night of July 25, 1956.

Also, the *Stockholm* was accused of being north of the

* See The Case of the *George S. Shultz*, 84F508.

usual eastbound lanes, but neither of the steamship lines which operated the *Stockholm* or the *Andrea Doria* ever agreed to join with the other nations in the North Atlantic Track Agreement, which merely suggests that the westbound lane, Track Charlie, should be taken while proceeding toward New York, and another course to the south should be followed eastward.

Down through the centuries man has had a desire to move faster, whether it be on foot, on horseback, in carriage, trains, ships or airplanes. Thus it is that speeds which were considered remarkable a century ago are regarded as ridiculously slow today.

One hundred years ago the average speed of liners in good weather or in fog was not over eleven knots, but the record-breaking voyage of the *United States* five years ago was at the unprecedented rate of 35.59 knots,* and more than a score of transatlantic vessels can operate within striking distance of this same speed.

Thus, not only is there relatively less chance of avoiding collision when ships are moving three times as fast as the speeds of a century ago, but when ships collide at the present rate of necessary scheduled speeds, they will be much more likely to sink after collision.

It is to be questioned whether the *Andrea Doria's* turbine engines could have been reversed in the limited time after the two vessels sighted each other before the crash. The *Stockholm,* with her piston diesel engines, had reversed probably within a few seconds of the sighting, but because of the momentum, even when she struck the Italian liner she must have been plowing along at better than fourteen knots.

---

* This voyage which lasted from July 3 to July 6, 1952 was at an average land speed of more than forty miles an hour!

Liners today have schedules which make no allowance at all for delays in fog. In this instance, for example, the accident took place at 11:22 at night on July 25. The *Andrea Doria* was scheduled to dock at 9:30 in the morning of July 27, almost two hundred miles away! Thus she would have had to maintain an average speed of over twenty-two knots to reach the Ambrose Lightship by 7:00 the next morning, and it is reasonable to believe that she must have been going close to twenty-two knots that night, and she may have been exceeding that speed just before the crash, fog or no fog.

When the collision occurred the *Ile de France* was over 220 miles away from Ambrose Lightship, which she had left at about 1:30 in the afternoon. She picked up the *Andrea Doria's* distress signals at approximately 11:22, or not quite ten hours after leaving Ambrose. Therefore, if she traveled 220 miles in less than ten hours, she must have been averaging around twenty-two knots through the same fog in which the other two craft collided.*

Although radar is a blessing to humanity, man has come into the habit of relying too much on this navigational aid. Strangely enough, if it had not been for radar, the two craft might not have noticed each other at all in the fog and probably would have sailed along without collision, passing by each other several miles apart.

The hearing in New York shortly after the disaster was held in the Foley Square Federal Courthouse where for

---

* In his superlative article, "Uneasy Lies the Head that Wears a Crown," published in the *U.S. Naval Institute Proceedings*, for January, 1957, former Matson Navigation Co. chief engineer John C. Carrothers stresses the point of relative speed. This veteran of 200 Atlantic crossings states that the *Stockholm's* admitted speed was eighteen knots. As both vessels, the *Ile de France* and the *Stockholm* left New York at the same time, how could the former vessel be 45 miles ahead of the Swedish craft if the *Ile de France* was proceeding at only seventeen knots?

the first time since the collision, the two opposing forces came together again. It was presided over by Judge Simon H. Rifkind.

Third Mate Carstens-Johansen of the *Stockholm* testified that he was standing the eight-to-twelve watch that July 25th night. He had been told by Captain Gunnar Nordenson to keep at least one mile from any other vessel. The third mate took radio bearings and echo sound bearings to find that he was a little northward of the dead-reckoning position they had plotted, probably pushed there by the current. He changed course a few degrees to adjust the drift. Returning to the wheelhouse, he looked in at the radar and discovered a ship about twelve miles away. The vessel was the *Andrea Doria*. When the stranger was ten miles off Johansen took a bearing on her and found that the *Doria* was two degrees off the port side of the *Stockholm*. It was then approximately 11:00. When six miles away the bearing of the echo sound was four degrees on the port bow and it was then five minutes past eleven. Finally, when about 1.8 miles away, Johansen actually sighted the oncoming craft. The *Doria* then showed two masthead lights and a weak red light. Following his captain's instructions, Johansen now ordered the course to be changed to "starboard, amidships, steady so," making his new course to the south. The *Stockholm* swung two points to starboard.

Unfortunately, aboard the *Andrea Doria*, also aware of the *Stockholm* by radar, the helmsman was swinging his great craft to the south as well. Johansen went out on the port wing of the bridge only to see with horror all the lights of the stranger's side coming toward him. The frightened officer on the *Stockholm* ordered full speed astern and hard starboard, but the crash followed almost immediately. Yet for some time, both liners had radar sights constantly on each other.

The hearing was transferred to the New York County Lawyers Association Building, where Captain Calamai, of the *Andrea Doria,* was given his chance to speak.

In the examination, Charles S. Haight, attorney for the Swedish line, asked the Italian captain why he had given no signal to abandon ship. Calamai explained that he wished to avoid panic if possible.

Haight then asked, "If you had given the regular emergency signal, six short blasts, followed by one short blast and the ringing of electric alarm bells, in your opinion would there have been panic among the passengers?"

Calamai answered in the affirmative. Haight also asked Calamai if he received any reports of passengers leaving the ship not by rope ladders or Jacob's-ladders, but by rope lines, and Calamai admitted that he knew passengers were leaving by various means. He also had heard of little Norma di Sandro being dropped into the lifeboat by her father.

Having spent thirty-nine years on the high seas, Captain Calamai was a sorrowing, defeated man when the hearing ended.

"I went to sea at an early age and all my life I loved it. Now I have nothing but hate left for the ocean."

On July 27 the Coast Guard announced that there had been 1,134 passengers and 572 members of the crew, or a total of 1,706 aboard the *Andrea Doria* at the time of the collision. As far as can be determined, all but about forty-five were saved.

Although it is an overwhelming thought, it is possible and even probable that some people were still alive when the *Andrea Doria* reached the bottom, about 240 feet below the surface of the ocean. Caught in staterooms sealed up by the crash, they may have lived for days at the bottom of the sea breathing the air imprisoned with them.

In January, 1957, both companies mutually agreed to abandon court action to fix blame for the collision. On February 15, 1957, the last day for filing them, the total number of claims was announced as 1565 and involved more than $116,000,000. Both vessels were partly covered by insurance.

Personal danger and loss of life on the *Andrea Doria* has pushed into the background the fact that millions of dollars' worth of cargo and valuables owned by passengers went down with the ship. Priceless paintings and statues created by Italy's finest artists decorated the interior of the ship. All now lie at the bottom of the Nantucket Sea.

There are many illusions which the average person fosters concerning a vessel which sinks. The most common misunderstanding is that anyone is allowed to attempt her salvage merely because she is at the bottom of the ocean. Actually, title to a wrecked ship always remains with the owner until changed by his own act or by the law. On July 29 the Italian Line announced it was not planning to abandon ownership of the *Andrea Doria*. One prominent deep-sea salvage expert has already guaranteed that he can bring the *Andrea Doria* up in a relatively short time.

The conclusions of the average mariner concerning this needless marine tragedy are many. Down through the years man has come to place too much emphasis on the inventions which he perfects. Radar, for example, should never take the place of human intelligence. It should merely supplement man's mind on the high seas. One must allow for human error, of course, but man oversteps his ability to cope with his own intelligence when he relies exclusively on the machines which he himself has invented.

As I have often stated before, a great marine disaster causes many people momentary wonder as to how such a calamity could happen. For ninety days or so after a sea tragedy the general public has its say in the newspapers and journals of the period. Then, the inevitable lassitude creeps in, and only those with a fixed purpose in the matter are left "crying alone in the wilderness" for reforms in maritime procedure. And so it goes until the next disaster.

I wish I had enough faith to say that shipping firms have taken or will take steps to remedy the custom of keeping schedules at all cost, which contributed so much to the loss of the *Andrea Doria*. However, down through the years there has been nothing to alter the average mariner's opinion as to what shipping firms will do. He feels that the line for which he works will not willingly change its rules to allow the speed of liners to be slowed for safety's sake. Unfortunately, because of the increased speed of travel, time has only accentuated the operating dangers to which the sea captains on the luxury liners are exposed.

Why do the shipping firms consider it so disastrous for a passenger liner to run even an hour or so behind schedule? It is because each hour of delay, in this mad frenzy of transportation speed, airplane competition and quick turnabouts, means extra costs amounting to tens of thousands of dollars. Whenever a luxury liner ties up at her pier, fuel barges, supply boats, provision trucks, stevedores, porters and customs officers are there waiting, and delays are extremely expensive.

What will be done to avert a similiar disaster in the future? Possibly now the shipping lines may take a first step forward toward humanizing their schedules in fog and storm. Otherwise, it will be merely a matter of time before you have the answer to the question which responsible maritime officers the world over are asking themselves: When will we have the next *Andrea Doria* disaster?

Meanwhile the stricken vessel has already become a part of the legends of the New England coast.

OUR FIRST NAVAL BATTLE

In 1762 the area around Machias, Maine, attracted the attention of several residents of Scarboro. Because of fire and drought on their own farmlands that autumn, they were searching elsewhere for hay and a possible site for lumbering operations.

Along the banks of the Machias River the visitors found a great abundance of salt hay. Moreover, a virgin forest of pine trees stood nearby, which seemed to stretch endlessly into the distance. Delighted by their discovery, they returned to their homes, having decided to settle permanently at the new location as soon as they could make the necessary arrangements.

Early the next spring they moved to Machias. Each succeeding year brought additional settlers so that by 1770, when a township grant had been secured, there were more than eighty families in the area. One by one sawmills were built, and soon there were five active mills working in the region. Trading in lumber with Boston and other colonies prospered from the very start.

In 1765, Morris O'Brien and his six sons had come to Machias from Scarboro. In company with several others they built the first double-saw mill, naming it the Dublin Mill in memory of O'Brien's former home in Ireland. Although the tiny settlement at Machias was more than 250 miles even from Falmouth (now Portland), the contacts which the lumber captains made with both Maine's largest seaport and Boston kept them abreast of the times.

Early in the spring of 1775 a group of prominent Machias citizens gathered in the Burnham Tavern. Having heard of the Battle of Concord and Lexington, they were anxious to discuss the critical news with one another and decide on a policy of action. Benjamin Foster proposed that a Liberty Pole be erected, and the other men approved heartily. A Committee of Safety was then suggested, but to make it official, the actual formation of the committee was postponed until the following day when the town could meet at a public gathering.

The meeting was held and the committee chosen. Before sunset that same day a tall pine-tree pole had been erected in the public square. Men, women and children congregated beneath it to pledge their property, their honor and even their life in the defense of their rights.

Meanwhile the plans of Captain Ichabod Jones were to have serious results in Machias. On June 2 two lumber vessels owned by the captain anchored off the settlement to be loaded. They were the *Unity* and the *Polly*. Captain Jones commanded the *Unity*, while his friend, Captain Horton, was master of the *Polly*.

Captain Jones, whose family had been prevented from returning to Boston from Machias because of the Boston Port Bill, was in a difficult situation. He had bought a residence in Machias, but his furniture was still in Boston. Wishing permission to get his household goods to his new Machias home, he had gone for help to Admiral Graves, in command of Boston Harbor.

The admiral told the captain that if he would bring to Boston two shiploads of lumber he would be allowed to take back his furniture. As a safety measure, Admiral Graves promised to send the armed schooner *Margaretta* with the vessels to Machias, thus insuring that the lumber would be loaded without trouble. Captain Jones agreed, and now the armed British schooner *Margaretta* stood by the *Unity* and *Polly* at anchor.

Jones went ashore to solicit lumber for his two schooners, but he did not get very far in his plans. The people of Machias not only were suspicious of his armed escort, but they resented the whole plan. Captain Moor of the *Margaretta* also had gone ashore to seek lodging for his fiancée and her chaperone during their stay. He found suitable apartments at the residence of Stephen Jones, where he left the two ladies. Returning to the wharf, Moor walked by the Liberty Pole.

"That pole must come down," he remarked to a group of men and women who were standing nearby, but he was firmly told that the pole would not be removed. Although gentlemanly in his manner, Moor announced that he would be forced to go aboard the *Margaretta*, train his guns on Machias and cannonade the town if the Liberty Pole were not taken down.

About to return to his vessel to execute this action,

Moor was hailed by Ichabod Jones, who was desperately anxious to prevent trouble. He implored the British commander to wait until a town meeting might be held, which he assured him could be persuaded to vote to remove the Liberty Pole. Moor finally agreed to suspend any retaliative measures.

That very afternoon the Committee of Safety met and recommended a town meeting for the next day. However, the members of the committee did not agree with Captain Jones, for they were certain that the vote would be overwhelmingly against the removal of the pole.

The Committee of Safety discussed plans for defense in case of attack. Deciding to recruit the help of other villages, they sent messengers at once to the nearest settlements, one at Chandler's River, now the town of Jonesboro, and the other at Pleasant River, an area now absorbed by the towns of Columbia and Addison.

Finally on June 10, the people of Machias voted unanimously to retain the Liberty Pole. On Sunday, June 11, finding out that Captain Moor was planning to attend the local church, several young men decided to take him prisoner.

As the religious services progressed, Captain Moor happened to glance out of the open church window. He saw to his consternation that several men were crossing the river below, each of them armed with a gun. They were residents of Chandler's River, arriving in answer to the pleas of the Machias Committee of Safety.

Fearing trouble, the English sea captain decided to act at once. He stood up in church, moved to the open window beside him and climbed out onto the grass. This unusual act left the congregation in an uproar, and several men left the meetinghouse. However, by walking rapidly, Moor reached his boat without being molested. He was quickly rowed out to his vessel which was soon moving down the river under sail.

True to his promise to cannonade the town, Captain Moor had several warning shots fired in the general direction of Machias. They were carefully aimed to do no damage, however, particularly as his wife-to-be and her chaperone were still in the town.

The Britisher sailed his schooner about a league downstream, where he foolishly anchored under the shelter of a high bank. Townspeople, noticing his vessel's mast, hastened to a location directly over the schooner where they aimed their muskets at the *Margaretta*. Hailing her captain, they ordered him to surrender.

Moor refused and again renewed his threat to fire on the town. But he weighed anchor, and the *Margaretta* ran out into the bay.

Back in Machias scant attention was paid to Captain Moor's threat to bombard the town. Instead, a meeting of the male residents was held in a field near O'Brien Brook to plan what should be done. Some of the men assembled there claimed that should an attack on the *Margaretta* actually be made, then Captain Moor would probably have to bombard the town in retaliation. Another argument was that as the Battle of Concord and Lexington had already been fought, it was their duty to follow the example of the Massachusetts men and openly resist the British.

At length, Benjamin Foster, weary of the discussion, went over to the brook which ran through the field, and stepped across it, inviting all who were in favor of capturing Captain Jones' sloops and the *Margaretta* to follow him. The response was unanimous in favor of his proposal.

All that afternoon groups had been arriving from the other settlements with guns, axes, pitchforks and scythes. Realizing that many of them would run out of ammunition should the battle last any length of time, two young girls at Chandler's River performed a heroic feat.

Seventeen-year-old Hannah and fifteen-year-old Rebecca Weston, sisters-in-law from Chandler's River, gathered about forty pounds of lead for musket bullets but found that there was no one left to transport it to Machias as all the men already had departed. The girls thereupon took matters into their own hands and tramped the whole distance to Machias with the priceless load tied in a pillow case, arriving well after midnight.

Early on Monday morning, June 12, before any tactical plans had been formulated, Wheaton and Dennis O'Brien met at the Machias wharf. They were soon joined by Peter Calbreth and a man named Kraft. The four men boarded the lumber schooner *Unity* and captured it without any serious opposition. A small group of witnesses on shore gave the four heroes "three rousing cheers," and soon a larger crowd was attracted to the wharf, among them Jeremiah O'Brien, "an athletic gallant man," to whom Wheaton described their exploit as soon as he came ashore. Encouraged by the ease with which Wheaton and the others had succeeded in their mission, O'Brien became enthusiastic about using the *Unity* to capture the *Margaretta*.

"My boys, we can do it!" he shouted, and everyone present rushed off the wharf to their homes to get arms and ammunition.

When the men returned to the pier, they had a wall

piece,* nineteen other guns, thirteen pitchforks and twelve axes. There were sixty charges of powder. Only sixty bullets had been molded by this early-morning hour from the lead which the Weston girls had carried through the forest, but with the axes and pitchforks the colonists decided they would sail out and attack the Britisher. For food they had "a few pieces of pork, a part of a bag of bread, and a barrel of water to drink."

Then came the moment when the crew was to be chosen. From the sixty-odd men assembled on the wharf their leader, Captain Jeremiah O'Brien, picked thirty-five of the huskiest to make the journey, including six members of his family. They faced a crew of forty on the British schooner.

Meanwhile, Benjamin Foster had already gone to East Falls to make ready another craft, the *Falmouth Packet,* and gather a company of men from that settlement. The vessels were to meet at the log boom known as the Rim. Unfortunately, the *Falmouth Packet* grounded in the East River en route, leaving the *Unity* to carry out the attack alone.

The *Margaretta* mounted sixteen swivels ** and four four-pound cannons, manned by seasoned fighters of the English Navy. However, in the colonists' favor was the British captain's anxiety to protect his fiancée who still remained ashore at Machias.

When Captain Moor saw the *Unity* approaching, he knew that it probably meant trouble. Crowding on all sail, he got underway and headed the *Margaretta* toward the open sea, hoping to avoid a conflict.

---

* A musket so heavy that it had to be rested on a stone wall or some similar object before it could be fired.
** Short, thick cannons, usually firing a one-pound ball, mounted on swivels which were placed on the vessel's rail.

Moor soon found that he was sailing by the lee and was, to quote an ancient chronicler, "obliged to jibe it (the mainsail) over to port. With a fresh breeze that was a task needing care, and yet, when he came to swing the boom across, he let it go back on the run, and it brought up against the backstays with such a shock that it was broken short off in the wake of the rigging."

Nearby in Holmes Bay was a merchant schooner, in command of Captain Robert Avery. After maneuvering toward Avery's craft, the desperate British captain boarded her and robbed the schooner of both her boom and her master. He fitted the boom on his own craft and impressed Captain Avery as pilot.

Still fearful of what lay ahead, Moor cut adrift all his boats for greater speed. He was desperate in his attempt to escape, but his efforts were all in vain. The *Unity* swiftly bore down on him, and the battle which James Fenimore Cooper has called the "Lexington of the Sea" was about to begin.

As the two vessels came together the English commander was the first to speak. Holding up his sea trumpet, he called out to Captain O'Brien that if the *Unity* came any closer he would have to open fire. O'Brien shouted back that there wouldn't be any trouble if Moor surrendered.

The British answered with the discharge of two cannon at the *Unity*. Within a few seconds there was a sharp exchange of cannon balls and bullets. One of the earliest shots killed a Machias man, after which an American named Knight fired the wall piece, killing the *Margaretta*'s helmsman and throwing the British seamen into confusion. They scrambled below and returned with muskets.

With no one at the helm, the *Margaretta* had swung

around, causing the *Unity* to crash into her, the American's bowsprit running through the Britisher's mainsail.

At that moment John O'Brien leaped aboard the *Margaretta's* quarterdeck. Expecting to be followed by his comrades, he was disconcerted when the two vessels parted, and he found himself alone with thirty-nine Britishers. As seven of the British crew fired at him and then charged him with their bayonets, O'Brien dove over the side. Swimming underwater, he came up near the *Unity*, where he was pulled aboard a few minutes later.

Again the *Unity* bore down on the luckless *Margaretta*. This time the grapnels were ready. As soon as the vessels were locked together, Captain O'Brien called for his men to follow him and jumped aboard the British craft.

Captain Moor, a brave man, singled O'Brien out for a private fight. Vainly throwing grenade after grenade at the American, Moor received a musket wound and fell to the deck. His second in command, a young midshipman, was so terrified at the fall of his commander that he retired below. The remainder of the fighting was short and decisive, but it cost the life of the impressed American pilot, Captain Avery.

Seeing that the British seamen had become disorganized with no one to command them, Captain O'Brien raised his voice.

"Do you all surrender?" he cried. "If you do, throw down your arms!" Muskets, handspikes and cutlasses clattered to the deck. The hour's engagement was over.*

The victorious Americans sailed the *Margaretta* back into Machias. The spoils of war taken from the British

---

* Although there is some discrepancy in the various reports, it is believed that there were three Americans killed and three severely wounded, while the British had three killed and about eleven wounded.

craft included two wall pieces, forty cutlasses, forty boarding axes, two boxes of hand grenades, forty muskets and
twenty pistols, with a good supply of powder and shot.

Captain Moor was carried to the home of Stephen
Jones, where his sorrowful bride-to-be had been awaiting
the outcome of the battle. He succumbed to his wounds
the following day, and she died of grief a year later.

Of course, when the British in Boston and Halifax found
out that O'Brien and his men had captured the *Margaretta,* they attempted swift retaliation. Two schooners,
the *Diligence* and the *Tapanagouche,* were sent down
from Halifax, but O'Brien sailed out and captured them
one at a time.

The British answer was to bombard Falmouth. When
the English Captain Mowat and his fleet appeared off Falmouth on October 16, 1775, he sent word ashore to remove "all human specie from the town" within two hours.
The bombardment began at nine thirty the following
morning, and according to Dodsley's *Retrospective View
of American Affairs,* no less than 3,000 shots were fired
into the town. When the British marines landed to "com-
pleat the destruction," they were repulsed with the loss
of a few men. Although Falmouth was laid waste, "with
130 dwelling houses, 278 stores and warehouses, and a
new large church destroyed," the British commander
acted with humaneness, and did not retaliate in any way
for the British marines who had been shot down. Not a
single resident of Falmouth was killed in the entire engagement.

PHANTOM SHIPS OF
NEW ENGLAND

MOST LEGENDS OF THE NEW ENGLAND COAST are based upon events which actually occurred in history, involving real people. This chapter, however, concerns phantom ships and sailors in the realm of the supernatural.

The legend of the Flying Dutchman is one of the most romantic of the many tales concerning spectral vessels current among sailors a century ago. It is also perhaps the best-known nautical legend. Novelists and poets have written it, while dramatists have twined it into plays, and it has been the subject of opera. The story is narrated with variations in nearly every maritime country, and folklore tales of similar phantom ships are abundant.

Below is quoted an accepted version of this now classic story, written by M. Jall:

"An unbelieving Dutch captain had vainly tried to round Cape Horn against a head-gale. He swore he would do it,

32

and, when the gale increased, laughed at the fears of his crew, smoked his pipe and drank his beer. He threw overboard some of them who tried to make him put into port. The Holy Ghost descended on the vessel, but he fired his pistol at it, and pierced his own hand and paralyzed his arm. He cursed God, and was then condemned by the apparition to navigate always without putting into port, only having gall to drink and red-hot iron to eat, and eternally to watch.

"He was to be the evil genius of the sea, to torment and punish sailors, the sight of his storm-tossed bark to carry presage of ill fortune to the luckless beholder. He sends white squalls, all disasters, and tempests. Should he visit a ship, wine sours, and all food becomes beans—the sailor's *bête noir*. Should he bring or send letters, none must touch them, or they are lost. He changes his mien at will, and is seldom seen twice under the same circumstances. His crew are all old sinners of the sea, sailor thieves, cowards, murderers and such. They eternally toil and suffer, and have little to eat or drink. His ship is the true purgatory of the faithless and idle mariner."

This is the same Phantom Ship, of which Scott sings:

> "Or of that Phantom Ship, whose form
> Shoots like a meteor through the storm;
> When the dark scud comes driving hard,
> And lowered is every topsail yard,
> And canvas, wove in earthly looms,
> No more to brave the storm presumes!"

New England, too, has her share of legends about spectral craft. In an Ojibway story, a maiden is about to be sacrificed to the spirit of the falls, by allowing her to drift over them in a canoe. But at the last moment, a spectral canoe, with a fairy in it, takes her place and serves as the sacrifice.

"While perchance a phantom crew,
In a ghastly birch canoe,
Paddled dumb and swiftly after."

Whittier writes of another American legend in the "Palatine"—the specter of a ship wrecked at Block Island, which is said to appear on the anniversary of its destruction when:

"Behold! again with shimmer and shine,
Over the rocks and the seething brine,
The flaming wreck of the Palatine."

It is a warning to sailors, too:

"And the wise sound-skippers, though skies be fine,
Reef their sales when they see the sign
Of the blazing wreck * of the Palatine."

It was long supposed that Dana's *Buccaneer* also described this *Palatine,* but the author says it is the sole work of his imagination.

In another poem, Whittier also alludes to:

"The spectre-ship of Salem, with the dead men
in her shrouds.
Sailing sheer above the water, in the loom of
morning clouds."

In an early and now scarce work, he tells the story of a spectral bark of Salem. In the seventeenth century a ship about to sail for England had as passengers a strange man and a girl of great beauty. So mysterious were their actions that they were supposed to be demons, and many

---

* I give the entire true story in my *Strange Tales from Nova Scotia to Cape Hatteras,* page 212.

feared to sail in the ship. The vessel embarked on a Friday and never reached her destination. After a storm that lasted three days, however, she reappeared, as narrated below:

> "Near and more near the ship came on,
>   With all her broad sales spread,
>   The night grew thick, but a phantom light
>   Around her path was shed.
> And the gazers shuddered as on she came,
>   For against the wind she sped."

On her deck were seen the forms of the young man and woman, and it took the prayer of the minister to dispatch this ghostly vision.

Whittier gives us another story of a phantom ship in "The Wreck of the Schooner Breeze." The young captain of the schooner visits the Labrador coast where, in a secluded bay, live two beautiful sisters with their mother. Both fall in love with the handsome skipper, who loves the younger one alone. She is confined in her room by her mother, just as she is to meet her lover and fly with him. Her elder sister, profiting by her absence, goes in her stead, and is carried to sea in the vessel. On learning the deception, the disappointed lover returns at once, but finds his sweetheart dead. The schooner never returned home, says the poem:

> "But even yet, at Seven Isle Bay,
>   Is told the ghastly tale
>   Of a weird unspoken sail.
>   She flits before no earthly blast,
>   With the red sign fluttering from her mast,
>   The ghost of the Schooner Breeze."

Possibly what is the best-known poem regarding phantom vessels was written by Whittier in 1866. It was called "The Dead Ship of Harpswell."

A letter of Whittier's,* written at Oak Knoll, Danvers, Massachusetts, in 1889, tells how he composed the poem:

My dear Friend:

Some 25 years ago I received from Miss Marion Pearl, daughter of the Rev. Mr. Pearl, a well-known clergyman of Maine, a letter descriptive of the people, dialects, customs, superstitions, and legends of Orr's Island where, I think the writer was a teacher. The legend of a spectre ship, as described in my poem, attracted me by its weird suggestiveness. Miss Pearl is now, I believe, the wife of an officer in the U. S. Army. I think I had a second letter from her confirming the story, but I fail to find it among my papers. I have no doubt that a quarter of a century ago the legend was talked of on the island, by the aged people. It was I am sure no invention of Miss Pearl. Perhaps it has died out now. The schoolmaster has been abroad since, and the new generation are ashamed of the fireside lore of their grandmothers.

I am glad thee are working in the line of these old stories. We need them all in this matter of fact age.

I am truly thy friend
John G. Whittier

It is true that the legend was "no invention" of Miss Pearl. The craft in question was the *Dash*, a topsail schooner of 222 tons, launched in 1813. Made over into a brigantine she sailed with a crew of 60 men under Captain John Porter in company with the *Champlain*. A gale caught the two vessels, and although the *Champlain*

---

* The letter is now in the Hollingsworth Collection at St. Paul's School, Concord, New Hampshire.

weathered the storm, the *Dash* was never heard from
again.

Whittier's poem, based upon this disaster, appears below together with the introductory stanza he wrote ac-
knowledging its source.

Introductory Stanza

Shifting his scattered papers, 'Here,'
    He said, as died the faint applause,
'Is something that I found last year
    Down on the island known as Orr's.
I had it from a fair-haired girl
    Who, oddly, bore the name of Pearl,
(As if by some droll freak of circumstance,)
    Classic, or wellnigh so, in Harriet Stowe's
      romance.'

The Dead Ship of Harpswell

What flecks the outer gray beyond
    The sundown's golden trail?
The white flash of a sea-bird's wing,
    Or gleam of slanting sail?
Let young eyes watch from Neck and Point,
    And sea-worn elders pray,—
The ghost of what was once a ship
    Is sailing up the bay!

From gray sea-fog, from icy drift,
    From peril and from pain,
The home-bound fisher greets thy lights,
    O hundred-harbored Maine!
But many a keel shall seaward turn,
    And many a sail outstand,
When, tall and white, the Dead Ship looms
    Against the dusk of land.

She rounds the headland's bristling pines;
    She threads the isle-set bay;
No spur of breeze can speed her on,
    Nor ebb of tide delay.
Old men still walk the Isle of Orr
    Who tell her date and name,
Old shipwrights sit in Freeport yards
    Who hewed her oaken frame.

What weary doom of baffled quest,
    Thou sad sea-ghost, is thine?
What makes thee in the haunts of home
    A wonder and a sign?
No foot is on thy silent deck,
    Upon thy helm no hand;
No ripple hath the soundless wind
    That smites thee from the land!

For never comes the ship to port,
    Howe'er the breeze may be;
Just when she nears the waiting shore
    She drifts again to sea.
No tack of sail, nor turn of helm,
    Nor sheer of veering side;
Stern-fore she drives to sea and night,
    Against the wind and tide.

In vain o'er Harpswell Neck the star
    Of evening guides her in;
In vain for her the lamps are lit
    Within thy tower, Seguin!
In vain the harbor-boat shall hail,
    In vain the pilot call;
No hand shall reef her spectral sail,
    Or let her anchor fall.

Shake, brown old wives, with dreary joy,
    Your gray-head hints of ill;
And, over sick-beds whispering low,
    Your prophecies fulfil.
Some home amid yon birchen trees
    Shall drape its door with woe;
And slowly where the Dead Ship sails,
    The burial boat shall row!

From Wolf Neck and from Flying Point,
    From island and from main,
From sheltered cove and tided creek,
    Shall glide the funeral train.
The dead-boat with the bearers four,
    The mourners at her stern,—
And one shall go the silent way
    Who shall no more return!

And men shall sigh, and women weep,
    Whose dear ones pale and pine,
And sadly over sunset seas
    Await the ghostly sign.
They know not that its sails are filled
    By pity's tender breath
Nor see the Angel at the helm
    Who steers the Ship of Death!

William Hutchinson Rowe quotes a poem on the same theme, which he found in a newspaper, possibly around 1900:

You have heard of the ship that sails the bay,
    With night for helmsman and death in tow,
And that glides to sea as he comes ashore
    And speeds on his errand of woe.

It was in the year of Eighteen-Twelve
    They launched the *Dash* from a Freeport yard,
She sails the bay as the 'Dead Ship' now,
    You have heard her doom from the Quaker bard.

She was manned by a crew of gallant lads
    As ever a vessel's deck had trod,
A score and a hundred of them all—
    And their fate is known to none but God.

They all belonged to the towns around,
    There were brothers and cousins and comrades too,
Full armed and equipped they put to sea,
    And the skies were never a softer blue.

But weeks and months and years sped on,
    And hearts grew hopeless and cheeks grew pale,
And eyes are dim that have watched so long
    To catch a glimpse of her home bound sail.

But when any of those who loved the lads
    Are ready to slip their moorings here
And sail away to the unknown port
    You will see the Dead Ship gliding near.

And the ship and the life go out with the tide,
    And the captain paused for awhile, then said
'They are most all gone and the Dead Ship soon
    Will come no more for the souls of the dead!'

LITHOBOLIA,
OR THE STONE-THROWING
DEVIL

Being an Exact and True Account (by way of Journal) of the various actions of infernal Spirits, or *Devils Incarnate* Witches, or both; and the great Disturbance and Amazement they gave to *George Waltons* Family, at a place called *Great Island,* in the Province of *New Hantshire* in New England, chiefly in throwing about (by an Invisible Hand) *Stones, Bricks* and *Brick-bats* of all Sizes, with several other things, as *Hammers, Mauls, Iron-Crows, Spits,* and other domestick Utensils, as came into their Hellish Minds, and this for the space of a Quarter of a Year. By R. C., Esq., who was a sojourner in the same Family the whole Time, and an Ocular Witness of those Diabolick Inventions. The Contents hereof being manifestly known to the Inhabitants of that Province, and Persons of other Provinces, and is upon record in his Majestie's Council Court held for that Province. 4to. Dedication 2, and pp.16. London: Printed and are to be sold by *E. Whitlook* near *Stationers-Hall,* 1698.

THE ABOVE TITLE PAGE was my introduction in 1942 to a small pamphlet printed in 1698 called *Lithobolia*. I was then in London, on duty with the Eighth Air Force. Anxious to examine this strange booklet, as I had been told it concerned one of the weirdest New England stories on record, I was disappointed when informed that because of the air raids all of the rare library books had been moved out of London. Later, when I transferred to the 12th Bomber Command at the time of the African invasion, I left London without having seen more than a copy of the title of the book, but since then I have been able to read it.

Lithobolia is the story of the Stone-Throwing Devil of the New Hampshire coast, a narrative written by an eyewitness to the affair, Richard Chamberline, who signed his 16-page effort with the initials "R.C." The volume is extremely rare. In the *Wonderful Providences* of Increase Mather there is an abridged version of *Lithobolia*, while a complete copy was reprinted in the *Historical Magazine* over 1. .ety years ago.

George Walton, the principal character in *Lithobolia*, lived in Portsmouth in the year 1682. He had incurred the hatred of an old woman of the neighborhood by taking from her a strip of land to which she laid claim. She was said to be a witch and was believed to be at the bottom of all the mischief that subsequently drove Walton's family to the brink of despair. This old lady had, in fact, told Walton that he would never peacefully enjoy the land he had taken from her.

Without warning, one still Sabbath night in June a shower of stones rattled against the sides and roof of Walton's house as unexpectedly as a summer hailstorm. As soon as the stone shower ended, the residents, who were in bed, hurriedly dressed and went out to see if they could find out who had been disturbing the peace and quiet of the family. It was then ten o'clock and a bright moonlight night. The family found that the gate had been taken off the hinges and carried some distance from the house, but nothing could be seen nor heard of the stone throwers.

While the family was outdoors in the moonlight, a second volley of stones whistled about their heads, driving them back into the shelter of the porch. The stones began to hit them there, however, and they quickly retreated inside, where, having bolted and barred all the doors, they awaited breathlessly the next assault of their assailants. Some of the family had been struck by the missiles, and all were thoroughly frightened.

A short time later the spectral stone shower began again, filling the room itself with flying objects which crashed through the windows to scatter the glass in every direction. Smashing down inside the chimney, the stones bounded and rebounded along the floor, while the family looked on in helpless amazement at what threatened to demolish the house over their heads. This bombardment continued intermittently for four hours.

While the stone shower kept up, Walton paced the floor of his room in great distress. Suddenly, a sledge hammer crashed through the ceiling, narrowly missed his head and fell at his feet, making a gash in the oaken floor. At the same moment the candles were swept off the table, leaving him in total darkness.

All evidence convinced the family beyond any doubt that the stones were hurled by demon hands. In the first place, some of those which were picked up were found to be hot, as if they had just been taken out of the fire. Secondly, even though several of them were marked, counted and put on a table, these same stones would afterward be found flying around the room again as soon as whoever had put them there had turned his back. Thirdly, the leaden crossbars of the windows were found to be bent out and not in, showing that the stones came from inside the house. Finally, some of the girls in the family were frightened out of their wits upon seeing a hand thrust out of a window, when to their certain knowledge there was no one in the room from which it came.

After Walton went to bed, though not to sleep, a heavy stone came crashing through his chamber door. He got up and locked the stone in his closet. He went back to bed, but the stone was taken out by invisible hands and carried with a great noise into the next room. At this moment the spit flew up the chimney, and came down again, without any visible human agency involved.

This queer activity continued from day to day with an occasional respite. Wherever the master of the house showed himself in the barn, the field or elsewhere, by day or by night he was sure to receive a volley. No one who witnessed this phenomenon doubted for a moment that all these acts proceeded from the malevolence of the witch.

Unusual to a high degree were some of the pranks of the demon. Walton had a guest staying with him, Richard Chamberline, who became the faithful recorder of what happened while the storm of stones continued to rain down upon the doomed dwelling.

One night, in order to soothe his mind, Chamberline took up a musical instrument and began to play. Immediately "a good big stone" appeared to join in with a dance while the player looked on in amazement.

Among other tricks performed by the mischievous spirit who had taken up its unwelcome residence among the family was that of moving a cheese from the press and crumbling it over the floor. The iron used in the press was later found driven into the wall, and a kettle hung upon it. Several cocks of hay that had been mowed near the house were adroitly hung upon trees nearby, and bunches of it were twisted into wisps which were stuck up all about the house kitchen.

The narrator of all these unaccountable doings admits that certain skeptical persons persisted in believing that any or all of them might have been the deeds of human beings; but this man who wrote the story 259 years ago left no doubt about his conviction that a spirit was at work.

We now quote directly from *Lithobolia:*

"After this we were pretty quiet, saving now and then a few stones march'd about for exercise, and to keep (as it were) the Diabolical hand in use, till July 28, being Friday, when about 40 stones flew about, abroad, and in the house and Orchard, and among the trees therein, and a window broke before, was broke again, and one Room where they never used before.

"August 1. On Wednesday the window in my ante-chamber was broke again, and many stones were plaid about, abroad, and in the house, in the daytime, and at night. The same day in the morning they tried this experiment; they did set on the fire a pot of Urine, and cooked pins in it, with design to have it boil, and by that means to give punishment to the witch or wizard, (that might be the wicked Procurer or Contriver of this stone affliction) and take off their own; as they had been advised. This was the effect of it:

"As the liquor began to grow hot, a stone came and broke the top or mouth of it, and threw it down, and spilt what was in it; which being made good again, another stone, as the pot grew hot again, broke the handle off; and being recruited and fill'd the third time, was then with a third stone quite broke to pieces and split, and so the operation became frustrate and fruitless.

"On Friday, the 4th, the fence against Mr. Walton's neighbour's door, (the woman of whom formerly there was great suspicion, and thereupon examination had, as appears upon record;) this fence being maliciously pull'd down to let their cattle into his ground; he and his servants were pelted with above 40 stones as they went to put it up again; for she had often threatened that he should never enjoy his house and land.

"Mr. Walton was hit divers times, and all that day in the field, as they were Reaping, it ceas'd not, and their fell (by the men's computation) above an hundred stones. A woman helping to reap (among the rest) was hit 9 or 10 times, and hurt to that degree, that her left arm, Hip, thigh, and leg were black and blue therewith; which she showed to the woman, Mrs. Walton, and others. Mr. Woodbridge, a divine, coming to give me a visit, was hit about the hip, and one Mr. Jefferys a Merchant, who was with him, on the leg. A window in the kitchin that had been much batter'd before, was now quite broke out, and unwindow'd, no glass or lead at all being left: a Glass Bottle broke to pieces, and the Pewter dishes (about 9 of them) thrown down, and bent.

"On Sunday, being the 6th, there fell nothing considerable, nor on Monday, (7th) save only one of the children hit with a stone on the Back. We were quiet to Tuesday the 8th. But on Wednesday (9th) above 100 stones (as they verily thought) repeated the Reapers disquiet in the corn-field, whereof some were affirm'd by Mr. Walton to

The death throes of the *Andrea Doria*. Pulitzer Prize winning photograph by Harry Trask. (*ch. 1*)

Sailors sight a phantom ship on the open sea. *(ch. 3)*

General Israel Putnam, hero of Chelsea Creek. *(ch. 10)*

Lady Eleanore Rochcliffe with her mantle of death. *(ch. 11)*

Captain Dodge and the mermaid. *(ch. 12)*

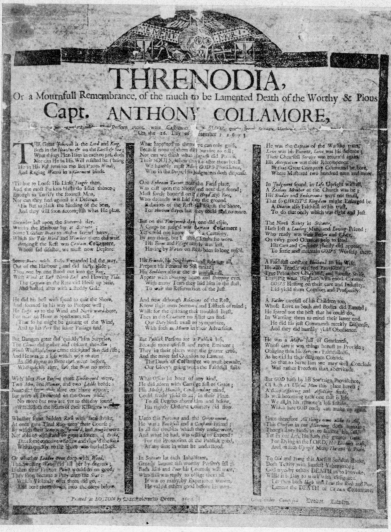

Courtesy of Massachusetts Historical Society

Photograph of the original broadside in which *Threnodia* first appeared. *(ch. 15)*

Photo by Edward Gluckler

The stranded *Etrusco* lashed by heavy seas off **Scituate**. (*ch. 16*)

Photo by Tony Spinazzola

Admiral Lebbeus Curtis (Ret.) who directed the salvaging of the
Etrusco. (ch. 16)

The wreck of the *Minerva* off Marshfield. (*ch. 17*)

The Scituate life savers on their way to the scene of the *Edward H. Norton* disaster, 1888. *(ch. 18)*

Courtesy of Carl C. Harris

The wreck of the *Edward H. Norton* at Scituate. *(ch. 18)*

Skin divers Edward Rowe Snow and Jerry Thomas with a shield and piece of wood brought up from the wreck of the seventeenth century galleon off Marshfield. *(ch. 19)*

Edward Rowe Snow dives from White Horse Rock. (*ch. 21*)

The reconstructed bones of the seventeenth century wreck *Sparrow-Hawk* are exhibited on Boston Common. (*ch. 22*)

The burning of the *Gaspée*. (ch. 26)

The *Lexington* burns on Long Island Sound. (*ch.* 29)

be great ones indeed, near as big as a man's head; and Mrs. Walton, his Wife, being by curiosity led thither, with Intent also to make some discovery by the most diligent and vigilant Observation she could use, to obviate the idle Incredulity some inconsiderate Persons might irrationally entertain concerning this venefical Operation; or at least to confirm her own sentiments and Belief of it. Which she did, but to her cost; for she Received an untoward Blow (with a stone) on her shoulder. There were likewise two sickles bent, crack'd and disabled with them, beating them violently out of their hands that held them; and this reiterated three times successively.

"After this we injoy'd our former peace and quiet, unmolested by these stony Disturbances, that whole month of August, excepting some few times; and the last of all in the month of September, (the beginning thereof) wherein Mr. Walton himself only (the Original perhaps of this strange Adventure, as has been declared) was the designed concluding sufferer; who going in his Canoe (or Boat) from the Great Island, where he dwelt, to Portsmouth, to attend the Council, who had taken Cognizance of this matter, he being summoned thither, in order to his and the Suspect's Examination, and the Courts taking order thereabout, he was sadly hit with three pebble stones as big as ones fist; one of which broke his head, which I saw him show to the President of the Council; the others gave him that Pain on the Back, of which (with other like strokes) he complained then, and afterward to his death."

Richard Chamberline was anxious to have proof that his fantastic story was true. Therefore he had "Some Persons of note" who were then in the area, sign the document below as "substantial witnesses of the same stonery":

"These Persons underwritten do hereby attest the truth of their being Eye-witnesses of at least half a score stones that evening thrown invisibly into the field, and in the entry of the House, Hall, and one of the chambers of George Walton's, viz:

Samuel Jennings, Esq; Governor of West Jarsey
Walter Clark, Esq; Deputy-Governor of Road-Island
Mr. Arthur Cook
Mr. Matt, Borden of Road-Island
Mr. Oliver Hooton of Barbados, Merchant
Mr. T. Maul of Salem in New England, Merchant
Captain Walter Barefoot
Mr. John Hussey
And the wife of the said Mr. Hussey."

JONATHAN MOULTON

AND THE DEVIL

HAMPTON, NEW HAMPSHIRE, has as her legendary hero
General Jonathan Moulton. There are two distinguished
men of letters who were interested enough in his "devil-
ish" legend to record fragments of it for posterity, John
Greenleaf Whittier in 1843 and Samuel Adams Drake in
1881. Drake covers the earlier period of General Moulton's life from his meeting with the devil, while Whittier,
in his poem, "The New Wife and the Old" tells of Moulton's second marriage.

The first legend runs as follows. One day Moulton's
yearning to amass wealth suddenly led him to declare
that he would sell his soul for the possession of unbounded
riches. At the time he uttered the fatal declaration the
general was sitting alone by his fireside. Without warning a shower of sparks came down the chimney. Out of
the fireplace stepped a man dressed from top to toe in

black velvet and despite his astonishment, Moulton noticed that the stranger's ruffles were not even soiled by the cloud of soot in which he had descended.

"Your servant, General!" said the stranger. "But let us make haste, if you please, for I am expected at the governor's in a quarter of an hour," he added, picking up a live coal in his thumb and forefinger, and illuminating his watch with it.

Drake tells us how the general's wits began to desert him. Portsmouth was fifteen long miles from Hampton House, and his strange visitor talked, with the utmost unconcern, of getting there in fifteen minutes! His astonishment caused Moulton to stammer out,

"Then you must be the—"

"Tush! What signifies a name?" interrupted the stranger, with a deprecating wave of the hand. "Come, do we understand each other? Is it a bargain, or not?"

At the word "bargain" the general pricked up his ears. He had often been heard to say that neither man nor devil could get the better of him in a trade. He took out his jackknife and began to whittle. The devil took out his, and began to pare his nails.

"But what proof have I that you can perform what you promise?" demanded Moulton, pursing up his mouth and contracting his bushy eyebrows, like a man who is not to be taken in by mere appearances.

The fiend ran his fingers carelessly through his hair, and a shower of golden guineas fell to the floor and rolled to the four corners of the room. The general quickly stooped to pick up one; but no sooner had his fingers closed upon it than he dropped it with a yell. It was red hot!

The devil chuckled. "Try again," he said. But Moulton shook his head and retreated a step.

"Don't be afraid."

According to Drake, Moulton cautiously touched a coin again, and it was cool. He weighed it in his hand and then rang it on the table; it was full weight and true ring. Then he went down on his hands and knees and began to gather up the guineas with feverish haste.

"Are you satisfied?" demanded satan.

"Completely, your Majesty."

"Then to business. By the way, have you anything to drink in the house?"

"There is some Old Jamaica in the cupboard."

"Excellent! I am as thirsty as a Puritan on Election Day," said the devil, seating himself at the table and negligently flinging his mantle back over his shoulder so as to show the jeweled clasps of his doublet.

Moulton brought a decanter and a couple of glasses from the cupboard, filled one, and passed it to his infernal guest, who tasted it, and smacked his lips with the air of a connoisseur. Moulton watched every gesture. "Does your Excellency not find it to your taste?" he ventured to ask; having the secret idea that he might get the devil drunk, and so outwit him.

"H'm, I have drunk worse. But let me show you how to make a salamander," replied satan, touching the lighted end of the taper to the liquor, which instantly burst into a spectral blue flame. The fiend then raised the tankard to the height of his eye, glanced approvingly at the blaze —which to Moulton's disordered intellect resembled an adder's forked and agile tongue—nodded, and said, patronizingly, "To our better acquaintance!" He then quaffed the contents at a single gulp.

Moulton shuddered, for this was not the way he had been used to seeing healths drunk. He pretended, however, to drink, for fear of giving offense; but somehow the liquor choked him. The demon set down the tankard, and observed, in a matter-of-fact way that put his listener in a cold sweat: "Now that you are convinced I am able to make you the richest man in all the province, listen! Have I your ear? It is well! In consideration of your agreement, duly signed and sealed, to deliver your soul"— here he drew a parchment from his breast—"I engage, on my part, on the first day of every month, to fill your boots with golden elephants, like these before you. But mark me well," said satan, holding up a forefinger glittering with diamonds, "if you try to play me any trick, you will repent it! I know you, Jonathan Moulton, and shall keep my eye upon you. Beware!"

Moulton flinched a little at this plain speech; but a thought seemed to strike him, and he brightened up. Satan opened the scroll, smoothed out the creases, dipped a pen in the inkhorn at his girdle and, pointing to a blank space, said, laconically, "Sign!"

Moulton hesitated.

"If you are afraid," sneered satan, "why put me to all this trouble?" And he began to put the gold in his pocket.

His victim seized the pen; but his hand shook so that he could not write. He gulped down a mouthful of rum, stole a look at his satanic majesty, who nodded his head by way of encouragement, and a second time approached his pen to the paper. The struggle was soon over. The unhappy Moulton wrote his name at the bottom of the fatal list of names which he was astonished to see numbered some of the highest personages in the province. "I shall at least be in good company," he muttered.

"Good!" said satan, rising and putting the scroll carefully away within his breast. "Rely on me, General, and be sure you keep faith. Remember!" So saying, the demon waved his hand, flung his mantle about him, and vanished up the chimney.

Satan performed his part of the contract to the letter. On the first day of every month the boots, which were hung on the crane in the fireplace the night before, were found in the morning stuffed full of guineas. It is true that Moulton had ransacked the village for the largest pair to be found and had finally secured a brace of trapper's jackboots which came nearly up to the wearer's thighs; but the contract merely expressed boots, and the devil does not stand upon trifles.

Moulton rolled in wealth; everything prospered. His neighbors regarded him first with envy, then with aversion, at last with fear. Not a few affirmed that he had entered into a league with the evil one. Others shook their heads, saying, "What does it signify? That man would outwit the devil himself."

But one morning, when the fiend came as usual, what was his astonishment to find that he could not fill the boots. He poured in the guineas, but it was like pouring water into a rathole. The more he put in, the more the quantity seemed to diminish. In vain he persisted; the boots could not be filled.

The devil scratched his ear. "I must look into this," he reflected. No sooner said, than he attempted to descend; but in doing so he found his progress suddenly stopped. A good reason. The chimney was choked up with guineas! Foaming with rage, the demon tore the boots from the crane. The crafty general had cut off the soles, leaving only the legs for the devil to fill. The chamber was knee-deep in gold.

The devil gave a horrible grin and disappeared. The same night Hampton House was burned to the ground, the general only escaping in his shirt. He had been dreaming he was dead and in hell. His precious guineas were secreted in the wainscot, the ceiling and other hiding places known only to himself. He blasphemed, wept and tore his hair. Suddenly he grew calm. After all, the loss was not irreparable, he reflected. Gold would melt, it is true; but he would find it all—of course he would—at daybreak, run into a solid lump in the cellar.

The general worked with the energy of despair, clearing away the rubbish. He refused all offers of assistance; he dared not accept them. But the gold had vanished. Whether it was really consumed, or had passed again into the massy entrails of the earth, will never be known. It is only certain that every vestige of it had disappeared. Subsequently a new house was built around the old chimney which was all that remained of the old.

The second legend goes to the effect that upon the death of his wife under—as evil report would have it—very suspicious circumstances, the general paid his court to a young woman who had been the companion of his deceased spouse, and they were married. In the middle of the night the young bride awoke with a start. She felt an invisible hand trying to take off from her finger the wedding ring that had once belonged to the dead-and-buried Mrs. Moulton. Shrieking with fright, the bride jumped out of bed, thus awaking her husband who tried in vain to calm her fears. Candles were lighted and a search was made for the ring; but as it could never be found again, the ghostly visitor was supposed to have carried it away.

This story is the same that is told by Whittier in the "New Wife and the Old." He explained in a letter which he wrote to a granddaughter of General Moulton that this story was told to him many years before by an elderly lady who often visited at his father's residence.

Years later a lady spent a summer at the Moulton House, which is claimed to be haunted. The woman declared that "strange noises were heard in the rooms, the steps and the rustling dress of a woman unseen on the stairs." The Reverend Mr. Willet of Newburyport was sent for to pray the ghosts away. Finally in all seriousness the minister is said to have locked the specters in a closet and departed.

Whittier tells us that he gives the story, "as I heard it when a child, from a venerable family visitant."

Lightly from the bridal bed
Springs that fair dishevelled head,
And a feeling, new, intense,
Half of shame, half innocence,
Maiden fear and wonder speaks
Through her lips and changing cheeks.

Listless lies the strong man there,
Silver-streaked his careless hair;
Lips of love have left no trace
On that hard and haughty face;
And that forehead's knitted thought
Love's soft hand hath not unwrought.

"Yet," she sighs, "he loves me well,
More than these calm lips will tell.
Stooping to my lowly state,
He hath made me rich and great,

And I bless him, though he be
Hard and stern to all save me!"

While she speaketh, falls the light
O'er her fingers small and white;
Gold and gem, and costly ring
Back the timid lustre fling,—
Love's selected gifts, and rare,
His proud hand had fastened there.

God have mercy!—icy cold
Spectral hands her own enfold,
Drawing silently from them
Love's fair gifts of gold and gem.
"Waken! save me!" still as death
At her side he slumbereth.

Ring and bracelet all are gone,
And that ice-cold hand withdrawn;
But she hears a murmur low,
Full of sweetness, full of woe,
Half a sigh and half a moan;
"Fear not! give the dead her own!"

Ah!—the dead wife's voice she knows!
That cold hand whose pressure froze,
Once in warmest life had borne
Gem and band her own hath worn.
"Wake thee! wake thee!" Lo, his eyes
Open with a dull surprise.

In his arms the strong man folds her,
Closer to his breast he holds her;
Trembling limbs his own are meeting,
"Nay, my dearest, why this fear?"
"Hush!" she saith, "the dead is here!"

"Nay a dream,—an idle dream."
But before the lamp's pale gleam
Tremblingly her hand she raises.
There no more the diamond blazes,
Clasp of pearl, or ring of gold,—
"Ah!" she sighs, "her hand was cold!"

When the general died and was buried, strange rumors
began to circulate that he had been seen hovering over
his old mansion in company with the devil. To quiet
these rumors his grave was opened, but when the lid was
taken from the coffin it was found to be empty.

A REAL NEW HAMPSHIRE WITCH

FOR WELL OVER A QUARTER CENTURY Eunice Cole, alias Goody, the witch of Hampton, New Hampshire, actually terrorized the residents who lived in and around that seacoast town. Her very name, Goody Cole, was used to insure the quietness of little children or hurry the feet of truant boys toward school. She was often thrown into prison for deeds which she was said to have accomplished by her witchcraft, and time and again she was brought before the local magistrates.

What was a witch in those awesome days? What terrible beings were these creatures, the fear of whom filled the minds of so many New Englanders for most of the last half of the seventeenth century?

Legally defined, "A witch is a person who hath conference with the Devil to consult with him or to do some act." *Devil* is a diminutive from the root *div*, whence also comes *divine*, and *devil* actually means "little God."

Although the Salem witchcraft episode of 1692 has created a great impression on all America, actually only a score of so-called witches lost their lives, a relatively small number compared with an estimated 42,000 executions of witches in Europe.

Nevertheless, as Marion L. Starkey so expertly tells us, it is hard for the average person to understand what happens to millions of people when religious or emotional frenzy overcome them. New Hampshire's part in witch hunts has not been given the importance which it possibly deserves and the story of Goody Cole is a case in point.

Goody Cole attracted the attention of the general New Hampshire populace in the year 1656 when she was first prosecuted for her witchlike behavior. Thrown into prison again and again, she soon became an outcast, and her little hovel down on the Hampton shore was shunned by all.

One of the worst deeds for which Goody was allegedly responsible occurred around the middle of the seventeenth century.

On a very hot summer day a "goodly company" of young people had sailed down the winding Hampton River on a fishing trip. Full of life, they were impatient to reach the sea where they could put out their lines.

As the vessel started to round the point they could see the hut of Goody Cole, and noticed the witch herself sitting out in front of the building, spinning yarn. A witness on shore saw one of the more daring girls climb into the shrouds.

"Fie on the witch," she shouted at the unfortunate woman.

"Oho," answered Goody from the shore. "You are very brave today, but I hear the little waves laugh and tell me that your broth that awaits you at home will be very, very cold!"

"Don't bother the witch," the captain admonished, as others in the party began to taunt the woman now standing on the edge of the shore. "It'll bring us no good at all!"

As young people often do, in spite of the captain's warning they kept up their jibes until the hut and its owner had vanished into the distance. By then the sloop was off Star Island, a favorite fishing spot on the Isles of Shoals, located about nine miles out to sea from the New Hampshire mainland.

The captain ordered the anchor put over and the sails furled. The sloop swung around into the light wind which had started to blow, and the young folks began getting their bait ready, opening clams and cutting up worms. Within two hours there was a satisfactory pile of fish on the deck, and the cook had come from below to choose some choice samples for the chowder which all aboard would soon enjoy.

Suddenly there was heard the sound of distant thunder. The captain, at once deeply concerned, ordered the anchor weighed and the sails unfurled. Fishermen ashore at Star Island watched as the sloop began sailing toward the shelter of the Isles of Shoals Harbor.

But it was too late. The helpless islanders saw a veritable wall of wind and rain approaching the vicinity. Striking the starboard side of the sloop, it shut out all visibility the moment it hit. Continuing, the rain squall smashed across Star Island, forcing the inhabitants to run for shelter.

The wind blew in terrible force for forty minutes, and then the sun came out again in the western sky. The squall over, the islanders hurried outside, anxious to learn how the sloop was faring. They looked out upon an ocean devoid of sail, and there wasn't the slightest sign of the sloop anywhere. Hurrying out to one of their vessels, the islanders sailed for the spot where they had last seen the sloop just before the storm broke. Reaching the area, they found nothing, and none of the party was ever seen again, dead or alive. The ocean had swallowed them up completely.

Back on the New Hampshire shore Goody Cole also thought of the sloop which had sailed by her hut. The squall had driven her inside, but with the return of the sun she hobbled down to the shore and looked seaward. Her countenance was set in hard lines, and she scanned the water out toward the Isles of Shoals. Then she returned to her spinning wheel beside the hut and sat down, her face wet with tears.

"They are lost, boat and all! The Lord forgive me, for my words about the broth were true. They will never return."

John Greenleaf Whittier has described the final episode in this story of a witch and the sea:

> Suddenly seaward swept the squall;
>   The low sun smote through cloudy rack;
> The Shoals stood clear in the light, and all
>   The trend of the coast lay hard and black.
> But far and wide as eye could reach,
>   No life was seen upon wave or beach;
> The boat that went out at morning never
> Sailed back again into Hampton River.

For Goody Cole, however, death was not to arrive with such speed, and there were to be several more years of accusation and torture. In her wretched hut she was cast off from all former friends, and she soon found it impossible even to obtain enough to eat. Months would go by without anyone's noticing whether she was alive or dead.

In the year 1680, because of an incident in Hampton itself, the poor woman was brought from her hovel to appear before the Quarter Sessions. There she was told to answer to the charge of being a witch. After her testimony, it was decided by the court that there was "noe full proof." What alleged proof they could find, however, was enough to doom the woman.

For the satisfaction of the court, which still "vehemently suspects her so to be," and probably to humor the people of New Hampshire, some of whom had sons or daughters who went down in the summer squall years before, she was given a terrible punishment.

Goody Cole was taken to the jail, and a great lock and chain were secured to her leg. After a number of days had elapsed, the woman was allowed to return to her hut on the beach, but one day some time afterward, passers-by noticed that there was no smoke coming out of her chimney. Two brave souls visited the hovel, where they found her body.

We have all heard of the inhuman custom of driving a stake through the corpse of anyone supposedly beset with evil spirits. As far as is known, this deed was rarely carried out in New England, but Goody Cole was to suffer this final indignity. And so it was that the men of New Hampshire dug a great hole, five feet deep and six feet square outside the little hut of the witch of Hampton. Dragging her body across the sand and into the hole, they let it lie there while one of them strode over to the chopping block. There he fashioned a long stake, and put a sharp point on the end. Walking slowly toward the pit where the remains of Goody Cole were lying, he stepped down beside her body. Two others joined him, and the stake was driven into her heart.

Ten minutes later, the grim men of Hampton began shoveling loose sand over the lifeless remains of the alleged witch. They left no sign to mark the grave of Goody Cole, hoping to discourage other witches in New England, but unfortunately, the witch hunt was only beginning.

OCEAN BORN MARY

IN THE YEAR 1814 there died at Henniker, New Hampshire, a very old woman whose story went back through the years to the days when the Scotch-Irish settlers were arriving in this country. It is only fair to state that there are now many versions of the story, but the original tale, unembellished by the passing of years, is the account which follows.

Around the year 1718 James Wilson and Elizabeth Fulton were married in Ireland and decided to go to America where they planned to settle. In June, 1720, they sailed away from Londonderry, Ireland, hoping that eventually they would reach Londonderry, New Hampshire.

From the very first the voyage was fraught with unexpected events. First the vessel sailed into stormy weather, then Elizabeth's baby was born prematurely. Finally, on July 28, when the weather moderated, a ship appeared on the horizon and began to chase the American-bound passenger craft. Soon there was no doubt that the pursuers were pirates.

The captain of the emigrant craft hastily called the crew and the leading members of the ship's company to a conference during which it was decided that resistance was useless, for there were not enough able-bodied men aboard to fight the pirates.

A few hours later, as the oncoming vessel fluttered her skull and crossbones from the mainmast, her crew fired a cannon across the bow of their victim, which immediately hove to, while the pirates put over several small boats.

In a short time the attackers were swarming aboard the passenger ship, shouting coarse piratical oaths as they scrambled over the rail. Then, like men trained to kill and plunder, they fell upon the awe-stricken crew and passengers, not one of whom offered any resistance. Soon every man was bound hand and foot, but so far no one had been killed. In a wild scramble for plunder such articles as could be transferred to the pirate vessel were piled together. Yelling and screaming the marauders rushed back and forth, unmindful of the entreaties of their victims.

While his followers were carrying on this lawless work, the captain of the buccaneers, whose hardened face revealed not the slightest sign of mercy, went below to search the officers' quarters, expecting to find some of his richest booty there. Bursting in the door, he discovered Elizabeth Wilson lying in the berth. The surprise of this piratical commander was evidenced by his long stare at the woman in the cabin bunk and the bundle at her side.

"Who are you, and why are you here?" he demanded.

The terrified mother uncovered the newly born infant and held the baby girl up for the intruder's inspection.

All appearance of his piratical character swiftly left him

and a kindly look swept over his countenance. The pirate advanced carefully to the mother's side.

"A girl?" he questioned.

"Yes," she answered timidly.

"Has she been named?"

"Not yet."

"Good."

Thereupon the pirate went back to the cabin door and ordered his men to stop all further action until he should return to the deck. Then, he again approached the side of the berth where the mother and her baby lay. All of his original thoughts of plunder and murder were forgotten. Almost reverently he took the tiny, unresisting hand of the baby in his own.

"If I may name this little girl for another I once knew, I promise life and safety to every passenger on this ship. On that condition, may I name the girl?"

"Yes."

Then the dark-browed outlaw of the sea, whose very name caused terror wherever it was spoken, bowed his head low over the mother and child while he whispered softly the name that seemed sacred to him: "Mary."

When he released the little hand, his tears were on it, while a strange light glowed from his countenance. A moment later he was gone, leaving the mother overwhelmed by the emotion the pirate had shown.

Upon reaching the deck, the outlaw ordered his men to unbind all the captives and restore the valuables to the places from which they had been taken.

Surprised, disappointed and grumbling, the pirates obeyed their leader, and a short time later the vessel was free of her unwelcome visitors. While unable to comprehend what had happened to make the attackers leave, the captain of the passenger craft gave orders to get under way.

The respite, however, was of short duration, for it was suddenly noticed that the pirate commander was coming back on one of the small boats! This time, however, he was alone with two oarsmen, so the fears of the passengers were somewhat quietened. As soon as he came on board, alone now, the pirate went directly below to the captain's cabin. Under his arm he carried a package of considerable size.

With mingled emotions Elizabeth Wilson watched him enter. To her surprise the visitor then unfolded before her startled gaze the most beautiful parcel of brocaded silk she had ever seen.

"Let Mary make her wedding gown from this," he said simply.

Then kissing the tiny hand of the now sleeping baby he stole silently out of the cabin.

The vessel continued on her voyage, eventually arriving in Boston where the passengers left the ship. The Wilsons carried out their plans and settled in Londonderry, New Hampshire.

That was well over two hundred years ago, and in that interval great changes have taken place in this country. For many years July 28 was religiously observed in the Wilson family out of remembrance to the christening of "Ocean Born" Mary, as she became known, a day of deliverance for herself and her friends from the pirates.

Left a widow in the course of time, Elizabeth Wilson married again. This time her husband was James Clark, a great-great-grandparent of Horace Greeley. As Mrs. Clark, she spent the remainder of her life in Londonderry.

On her eighteenth birthday Ocean-Born Mary became

the bride of Thomas Wallace and her wedding gown was made from the pirate's silk. Nor was she the only one to wear this wonderful dress, for although she had no daughter of her own it was handed down to granddaughter and great-granddaughter to be worn on similar occasions. Ocean-Born Mary lived the last years of her long and happy life in Henniker and her grave is in the cemetery there located close to the railroad station.

In the year 1946, L. M. A. Roy was living in the Ocean-Born-Mary House.

He informed me that the same pirate who named the Wilson girl later sailed up the Merrimac River and the Contoocook until he reached Henniker. The buccaneer had brought along his followers, slaves and carpenters, and there he built the Ocean-Born-Mary House. At the same time, according to Mr. Roy, he brought a large treasure along with him, which he buried in the vicinity. A short time later the pirate was found with a cutlass run through his body in the grove behind the mansion, and he was buried nearby. There is a large slab of granite which serves as a hearthstone in the kitchen of the house which the outlaw is said to have intended as his tomb.

When Ocean-Born Mary died in the Eagle Room of the Henniker mansion in 1814, she was ninety-four years of age. A visit to her house will well repay your time. Built after 1760, it is a typical sea captain's residence and a fragment of the original silk given to Ocean-Born Mary by the pirate is reputedly still on exhibition.

POCAHONTAS OR ENEWA?

THREE HUNDRED AND TWENTY-SIX years ago there died in an obscure English village a man who perhaps is as responsible as anyone for there being a Massachusetts or even a New England.

The only thing many people remember about John Smith is that he was saved from death by Pocahontas, the daughter of an Indian chieftain in Virginia. There persists, however, a legend that the event actually took place in New England and the girl's name was Enewa.

In order to understand the background of this New England legend it is important to know the location of some of the various tribes and villages of the Yankee red men.

When John Smith visited New England, which he named, it was before a great plague had decimated the Indians of that region. The shore tribes of southern Massachusetts and Rhode Island were the Pocassets. At the time of his visit to Boston a tribe known as the Massachusetts were located around Boston Bay. Their name came from "A hill in the form of an arrow's head," or the Blue Hills, and their territory extended from the Blue Hills to the Pokonoket region to the south. The influence of the Massachusetts tribe to the north and east reached the Pawtuckets who lived in the general region from Salem to Portsmouth, New Hampshire.

Then there were the Nipmucks who controlled the area of Essex County, part of Middlesex County and a section of New Hampshire. The Nipmucks were widely scattered and usually dominated inland areas to the west of the coastal regions.

West of the Hudson River were the ferocious Mohawks, and the Nipmucks near the Hudson had been absorbed by the more forceful Indians in that region. However, in what is now New Hampshire there were six large clans of Nipmuck Indians and a few smaller groups of no great importance. Those six tribes of Nipmucks were the Pennacooks, Agawams, Naumkeags, Piscataways, Accomintas and Newichawannocks. It is about Enewa, the Laughing Daughter of the Sachem of the Newichawannocks, and John Smith that our story is concerned.

The usual John Smith story concerns Pocahontas, the Princess of Werowocomoco, a tribe many hundreds of miles to the south of New England. Without question no Indian maiden in history is more admired than Pocahontas. She is always pictured as a fearless, beautiful, Indian girl. John Smith had fallen captive to the mighty Powhatan, the ruler of a vast confederacy of Indians. Smith, taken to a sacrificial rock, was about to have his brains smashed out when Pocahontas rushed forward and placed her own body between that of John Smith and the descending execution club.

The story goes that her father, the Chief Powhatan, after vainly attempting to reason with her, finally yielded and allowed the Englishman's life to be saved. Eventually, as historians tell us, Pocahontas married one of Smith's associates, John Rolfe by name, and crossed the ocean with him to spend the rest of her days in England.

The fact of the Pocahontas-Rolfe marriage is well authenticated and documented, but for those interested in the New England version of the tale, it was not the daughter of Powhatan who saved John Smith, but an Indian girl of the Piscataqua River.

John Smith made his first voyage along the New England coast in the year 1614, discovering Monhegan Island, where a tablet to his memory can now be seen. On his travels from Maine to New Hampshire, Smith reached the broad mouth of the Piscataqua River and was impressed by what he saw.

Anchoring his three vessels at the mouth of the river, he instructed his crew to lower his small boat over the side. Carefully choosing six of his bravest comrades, Smith started up the Piscataqua River on a voyage of discovery and exploration. It was one of those rare summer days "when all the world seems in tune." As the sound of the booming waves along the New England coast grew fainter and fainter the river began to narrow, and Smith admired the primeval beauty of his surroundings.

Unknown to him, however, his craft was advancing into an ambush. A large party of Newichawannock Indians had sighted his three vessels many hours before. Even then their own efficient fleet of war canoes was lying in wait for the small boat of the white man. As the John Smith party rounded a bend in the New Hampshire river a series of terrifying war whoops shattered the summer stillness, and the attack which followed overwhelmed the seven Englishmen. Quickly trussed up, they were taken to an Indian camp located a relatively short distance away on the banks of the river.

Here the chieftains gathered in council to discuss what they should do to these unfortunate intruders who had the audacity to invade the land of the mighty Newichawannocks. This brave warrior, John Smith, veteran of battles on three continents, did not betray in his countenance that he knew his position was relatively hopeless. The red men walked him to a young sapling and bound him there, tying his feet and hands with rawhide thongs.

A group of Indian braves stood at some distance from the tree, behind which was a boulder, and took turns shooting their arrows into the upper parts of the trunk where their victim was tied. Gradually their aim dropped lower and lower. A silent watcher of the affair was Enewa, the Laughing Daughter of the chief who ruled all the Newichawannocks. As the arrows approached the prisoner, she became increasingly nervous.

Suddenly, when an arrow actually parted the locks of hair at the top of Smith's head, Enewa could restrain herself no longer. Springing up from a hummock where she had been sitting she ran directly in the path of the flying missiles, rushed up to the Englishman and placed an arm around his shoulders. The sachem of the Newichawannocks, furious that his daughter should interfere with the proceedings, ordered his braves to pull the girl away.

Realizing that Smith would be killed should her father's orders be carried out, Enewa clung with desperation to the neck of the captain. After several unsuccessful attempts had been made to separate the girl from the captive, her father decided that a compromise was necessary. Motioning the Indian braves to step aside, he strode slowly toward his daughter. Enewa explained to her father that if Captain John Smith were killed, she would die with him.

The sachem of the Newichawannocks finally yielded and the captain was untied and released. Smith's crewmen were likewise set free. Later, after a council meeting between the white man and the Indians it was agreed that John Smith would explore no more toward the source of the Piscataqua River but return at once to his three waiting vessels.

The Indians agreed to paddle their canoes alongside the shallop of the white man. Eventually, when they reached the English craft, Smith invited the Indians aboard his ship, and Enewa enjoyed to the utmost the visit to the large vessel of the white man whose life she had saved.

When the moment came for parting the Indians and the whites exchanged gifts. At the final minute of farewell John Smith dressed himself in his finest military uniform and asked the girl who had saved his life what token she would like to have to remember him by. Greatly impressed by the attractiveness of his splendid uniform she indicated that nothing would please her more as a keepsake than one of his large bright buttons.

The gallant captain stepped back a pace and drawing his sword with a flourish, he held the brightest, gold-colored button firmly between the thumb and forefinger of his left hand. Of course it was the button over his heart. Then, with a quick stroke he severed it from his uniform and handed it to the happy girl.

Two hours later his fleet had rounded Ordiorne's Point

and vanished forever out of the life of the Laughing Daughter of the Newichawannocks.

In conclusion, let us quote from the pen of George Waldo Browne, one of the authorities who subscribe to this version of the legend:

> "John Smith modestly refrains from describing the parting with his brave young friend who had saved his life, but he gave her a bright button from his uniform, which it is safe to say she kept and cherished all of her life, which we trust was long and happy. And this is the true story of how John Smith's life was saved, not by Pocahontas, the Princess of Werowocomoco, but by Enewa, the Laughing Daughter of the sachem of the Newichwannocks."

9

THE UNWED MAID
OF MARBLEHEAD

CHARLES HENRY FRANKLAND was born in Bengal, India,
on May 10, 1716, the son of Governor Frankland of the
famous East India Company. A lineal descendant of
Oliver Cromwell, Harry, as he was called, came into possession of a considerable fortune at the age of twenty-
two.

Clever and handsome, Frankland was the eldest of his
father's seven sons. He was educated in French, Latin,
botany and even landscape gardening, and also had a remarkable knowledge of the leading literary figures of the
day.

In 1741, because of the transfer of Governor Jonathan
Belcher and the death of Boston Port Collector, John
Jekyl, during the same period, there were vacancies in
two important political positions in Massachusetts. The
Duke of Newcastle offered Harry both of them, but since
he was only twenty-four, his friend, William Shirley, fi-

nally was given the governorship while Harry became
Collector of the Port of Boston.

The society in which Frankland, now Sir Harry, moved
really set the fashions of the day, at least for the men. In
Boston he wore a brocaded vest, gold-lace coat, broad
ruffled sleeves, three-cornered hat, powdered wig, side-
arms and silver shoe buckles. Indeed he was a striking
figure.

One day his duties called him to visit the new but un-
finished Fort Sewall at Marblehead, overlooking Marblehead Harbor and Boston Bay. On his way Sir Harry
stopped for a drink at the nearby Fountain Inn. Entering
the inn, the baronet spied what apparently was a bare-
legged and barefooted child scrubbing the floor. Frankland looked again, and the child stood up to reveal herself
as a beautiful sixteen-year-old girl with "black curling
hair" and pretty dark eyes. Her name was Agnes, and she
had a musical voice which was sweet to hear. Frankland
was overwhelmed at once. Oliver Wendell Holmes describes the scene:

> A scampering at the Fountain Inn;
>   A rush of great and small;
> With hurrying servants' mingled din,
>   And screaming matron's call!
>
> Poor Agnes! with her work half done,
>   They caught her unaware,
> As humbly, like a praying nun,
>   She knelt upon the stair;
>
> A foot, an ankle, bare and white,
>   Her girlish shapes betrayed,—
> "Ha! Nymphs and Graces!" spoke the Knight
>   "Look up, my beauteous Maid!"

She turned,—a reddening rose in bud,
　　Its calyx half withdrawn;
Her cheek on fire with damasked blood
　　Of girlhood's glowing dawn!

He searched her features through and through
　　As royal lovers look
On lowly maidens when they woo
　　Without the ring and book.

"Come hither, Fair one! Here, my sweet!
　　Nay, prithie, look not down!
Take this to shoe those little feet,"—
　　He tossed a silver crown.

She flitted; but the glittering eye
　　Still sought the lovely face.
Who was she? What, and whence? and why
　　Doomed to such menial place?

A skipper's daughter,—so they said,—
　　Left orphan by the gale
That cost the fleet of Marblehead
　　And Gloucester thirty sail.

Frankland, much more impressed with the girl than he realized, having given her the piece of silver, mounted his horse and rode out toward Fort Sewall.

But the image of the sixteen-year-old Agnes stayed in his mind. The next chance he had he again stopped at the Fountain Inn, where he saw her for the second time without shoes and stockings. Frankland teased her about the money he had given her, and she blushed in return.

"I bought the shoes and the stockings," she replied, "but of course I keep them to wear to meeting." Frankland was so impressed with her personality that he decided to

do something about her education and social training, and
so he made a note to inquire about her. After locating
her parents, he soon was able to talk with them.*

Edward and Mary Surriage agreed that Sir Harry could
become the guardian of their daughter, and shortly afterward he took her up to Boston with him to put her in a
finishing school.

Agnes was taught reading, writing, grammar, music and
embroidery by Boston's best instructors, and all the time
that she learned her lessons she grew in both beauty and
maidenly charm, at the same time retaining her gift of
childish sweetness and simplicity. She was visited weekly
by her mother and the Marblehead pastor. Governor Shirley's wife, who was also interested in the girl, often had
her out to Roxbury and to Medford at the Royal Mansion.

After her education had been completed, however, and
Agnes had blossomed into a remarkably attractive young
lady, Harry Frankland fell in love with his ward, and she
returned his affections.

Perhaps in those days a baronet simply did not marry
a low-born ward from an inn. Possibly at first Frankland
did not realize what was happening. But the women of
social Boston were quick to understand that Agnes Surriage, the ward of Sir Harry Frankland, was now the object
of his love and that he had no intention of marrying the
girl.

Thus, although formerly Agnes had been received with
kindness by the most aristocratic people in Boston, the
ladies of the socially prominent group now turned her
away from all functions, because she was beloved but not
married. It was not long before Frankland also felt the

* Holmes is incorrect in stating that her father was dead at the time.

pressure of public opinion. For those of you who wish to study at close hand such sociological problems, Sir Harry's diary is still available in Boston.

The snubbing which the women gave both Sir Harry and Agnes eventually forced him to move out of town to Hopkinton, where the rector of King's Chapel, the Reverend Roger Price, sold him four hundred acres. There in 1751, Frankland completed the building of a great mansion.

Moving out to Hopkinton the following year, Frankland and Agnes began their life in the country. They had twelve slaves to give them every comfort. Harry was able to satisfy his horticultural whims, and great boxes of the latest books from England gave him much literary enjoyment, with the works of Swift, Addison, Steele, Richardson and Pope among his favorites.

Sir Harry had many guests, men who would often visit with him at the relatively close Wayside Inn, twelve miles from Hopkinton. Then they would ride out to his home and enjoy a wonderful selection of wines from his large cellar. He made a good friend of the local village rector and carefully observed "all the forms of his religion." He always treated Agnes with the complete respect to which a wife is entitled, but for some reason neglected the one act which would have made the union complete.

In 1754 business called Frankland across the ocean, and Agnes went with him. Arriving at his widowed mother's home, Sir Harry was accepted but Agnes was not, and the poor girl from Marblehead was subjected to social ostracism of the most humiliating form.

And so it was that Sir Harry and Agnes left England for Portugal as soon as the legal matters responsible for the visit were finished. Lisbon in those days was the capi-

tal of moral laxity and tolerated what has been called the
"*alliance libre.*"

On November 1, 1755, All Saints Day morning, at the
very moment when "beggar and priest, courtier and
lackey" were making their way through Lisbon with its
beautiful convents, its outstanding churches and royal
palaces, the entire city was devastated by the worst earthquake ever to hit Europe in modern times. Sixty thousand
people were killed by the falling buildings and the giant
caverns which opened up and swallowed them, while
scores of thousands more were injured in the disaster.*

The temblor came about ten o'clock in the day, just as
the *misericordia* of the Mass was being sung in the
crowded churches. At the time Agnes was at the apartment where they were staying, but Frankland was riding
in his carriage with another lady on his way to the religious ceremony. The ruins of several buildings fell upon
them, burying Sir Harry and the lady in his carriage, and
killing his horses. One large fragment entered the carriage roof and embedded itself in the body of the lady.

In her agony, with the heavy weight which had already
crushed her body still on her, she fastened her teeth onto
the red broadcloth coat which her escort was wearing, actually biting through the cloth and tearing his flesh.**
Frankland evidently suffered some terrible thoughts as he
lay there pinned under the wreckage, his body torn by
several injuries and his mind on possible death.

Meanwhile, back at the apartment where they were
living, Agnes had not been hurt. Quickly she gathered

---

* A great quay, with 3,000 persons on it was submerged *under* the bottom of Lisbon Harbor in a peculiarly horrible folding under and over
of the earth's surface during the shock.
** After a careful page-to-page scrutiny of Frankland's journal, I have
been unable to find this woman's name or even whether she survived.

together what money there was available and ran out on
the debris-laden streets. Her intention was to search for
her lover and help him if he needed it. While passing
down a main street, she suddenly recognized his an-
guished voice coming from the wrecked carriage, underneath a mass of rubble. Organizing a rescue group by
offering them gold, Agnes soon had a corps of workers removing the debris from the victims. Both the lady and
Frankland were finally uncovered and taken to a nearby
residence where a short time later Frankland called for a
priest.

While the priest was on the way, Harry told Agnes that
he had endured some bitter moments at the time he
thought that he was dying. He could wait no longer. He
had promised God to mend his ways and to atone to
Agnes, if God should allow him to live, and he was not
going to waste a moment in carrying out his pledge.

"Will you marry me, Agnes?" he asked. The records do
not state how long she took to reply, but in any case by
the time the priest arrived the two were ready for the
marriage ceremony.

Not only did the pair become husband and wife that
first day of November, 1755, but they were married again
aboard the next ship which sailed for England. This time
the service was performed by a clergyman of Frankland's
own church. The bridegroom's thoughts at the time as
stated in his diary were: "Hope my providential escape
will have a lasting good effect upon my mind."

Arriving back in England, Agnes was now given friend-
ship and affection instead of the aloofness she had endured before. Additional business matters made a second
visit to Lisbon imperative, and it was from Belem that
they sailed for America in April, 1756. Their arrival in

Boston was the cause of much rejoicing by the friends of both.

The couple stayed during the summer of 1756 at their Hopkinton home, but in October, Sir Harry purchased the famed Clarke mansion on Garden Court Street. The house was one of the great showplaces of Boston. It had inlaid floors, was three stories high and contained twenty-six rooms. The stairs were so broad and wide that Sir Harry often rode his pony up and down them with perfect safety. Such stunts were usually restricted to times when he entertained his friends at stag parties. It was on these occasions that he drank from his wine glass of double thickness which assured that he could remain sober long after most of his guests were under the table.

All of his friends were extremely happy that Frankland had finally married Agnes. On November 30, 1756, Edmund Quincy wrote him that "I hope yr goodness will excuse an epistolary tender of my sincerest complements on ye pleasing occasion. . . . *Tel qu'il est*, permit me ye pleasure of assuring you that it is accompanied by the sincerest regard of, Sir, Yr. most obedient & very humble S't. E.Q."

As the years went by, however, Frankland did not enjoy the New England winters. Finally he decided to accept the post of consul general back at Lisbon. The entries in his diary speak of what he planned to purchase in London for the Lisbon stay, and include "silver castors; wine glasses like Pownal's, two turreens; saucers for water glasses, . . . jelly and syllabub glasses; fire-grate; . . . stove for flatirons; glass for live flea for microscope; Hoyle's Treatise on Whist; Dr. Doddridge's Exposition on the New Testament, 16 handsome chairs with two settees and 2 card tables, working table like Mrs. F. F. Gardner's."

Sir Harry returned to Boston and Hopkinton briefly in 1763, but he found our wintry east winds too boisterous, and the following year he went back to England and "took the treatment" at Bath, drinking copious amounts of the waters.

His comments during that period indicate that he was anxious to keep himself "calm and sedate." Although only around fifty at the time, he had already become bitter toward some of his associates. His remarks follow:

"I live modestly and . . . do not entertain a number of parasites who forget favors the moment they depart from my table."

Shortly afterward he became bedridden and died at Bath on January 2, 1768, at the age of fifty-two, where he was buried in the parish church.

Agnes returned to Boston and moved out to Hopkinton with her sister and her sister's children. There she stayed, peacefully, "among her flowers, her friends and her books until the outbreak of the Revolution," according to Mary Caroline Crawford.

Then on May 15, 1775, after the historic encounter at Lexington and Concord, Lady Frankland moved to Boston, taking with her among other things, "6 wethers; 2 pigs; 1 small keg of pickled tongues; some hay; 3 bags of corn; and such other goods as she thinks proper."

Arriving in Boston, she watched the Battle of Bunker Hill from her mansion, and later helped bandage the injuries of the British soldiers wounded there. Of course, by then she was a Tory in sentiment, but whether or not she thought of the old Marblehead days and her American friends at the Fountain Inn, history does not state.

About the time of the evacuation of Boston she moved back to England. In 1782 she married a rich banker of

Chichester by the name of John Drew. One year later she died.

There is no known picture of this beautiful lady available, but it is certain that she must have been lovely, and she stands as a truly legendary, romantic figure of the Massachusetts coast.

PUTNAM, THE INCREDIBLE

ISRAEL PUTNAM WAS BUILT of the material of which legends are made. More a soldier than a strategist or tactician, Putnam had within him the inherent quality of a leader that made men follow him blindly. There is controversy about almost every part of his life. The place of his birth, originally thought to be Salem Village, is now known as Danvers, Massachusetts, and even the location of his grave is obscure. Paradoxically, one of his great achievements, the winning of the Battle of Chelsea Creek, which took place before the Battle of Bunker Hill in which he also fought, has been almost entirely ignored by historians of the Revolutionary War.

At the time, the British in Boston were greatly in need of meat; in fact, many of them were becoming ill because of the inadequate diet. Philip Freneau, the spirited song writer of the Revolution, tells us of the laments of General Gage; who was then the military commander of Boston.

Three weeks, ye god! nay, three long years it seems,
Since ROAST BEEF I have touched, except in dreams.
In sleep, choice dishes to my view repair;
Waking, I gape, and champ the empty air.
On neighboring isles, uncounted cattle stray.
Fat beeves and swine,—an ill defended prey;
These are fit vision for my noon-day dish;
These, if my soldiers act as I could wish,
In one short week would glad your maws and mine;
On mutton we will sup, on roast beef dine.

Gage, however, had not figured on Israel Putnam who had also noticed the cattle and sheep on the neighboring islands of Boston Harbor. In fact, on May 14, 1775, the Committee of Safety had passed a resolution, excerpts from which follow:

"Resolved, as the opinion of this committee, that all the live-stock be taken from Noddle's Island, Hog Island, Snake Island, and from that part of Chelsea near the sea-coast, [Chelsea then included the area now known as Winthrop and Revere] and be driven back . . ."

And so it was that whereas the first battle of the Revolution at Concord and Lexington was fought over munitions, the second real battle of the Revolution, now almost forgotten, was fought over food and resulted in more deaths than the opening conflict.

At eleven o'clock on the morning of May 27, 1775, a little more than a month after the Battles of Concord and Lexington, Israel Putnam gave Colonel Stark orders to go to Hog Island.* Instructed to capture all animals in the vicinity, Colonel Stark crossed from the mainland at Chelsea by a ford in the creek and removed four hundred

---

* Now known as Orient Heights, part of East Boston.

sheep. While at Hog Island he and his men were seen by a number of British marines stationed on Henry Howell Williams' farm at Noddle Island, now East Boston. A short skirmish followed, but no one was killed.

However, the noise of gunfire was heard by the British warships in the harbor. Colonel Stark had taken advantage of the low tide, for there was a ford both at the Chelsea-Hog Island crossing and at the Hog Island-Noddle's Island crossing, each of which was knee-deep at low water for a brief period.

The detachment, composed of New Hampshire and Massachusetts troops, included about six hundred men, which was much larger than the number of Americans who had fought at Concord and Lexington five weeks before. After making sure that the four hundred sheep were safe in Yankee hands, the Americans returned to Hog Island and then crossed over onto Noddle's Island to find whatever cattle they could there. To prevent the British getting them, they killed a few horses and "divers horned cattle," and managed to start a herd toward Hog Island. Suddenly they heard a cannon shot. It was a signal gun, fired from the armed British schooner *Diana,* then lying off the Winnisimet ferry ways.

Shortly afterward they observed a red flag hoisted to the masthead of the *Diana.* As the tide began to come in, the schooner weighed anchor and began sailing together with an armed sloop up Chelsea Creek. Their plan was to cut off the return of the American soldiers. The *Diana's* guns consisted of four six-pounders and twelve swivels. In addition to the schooner and the sloop, which was relatively well armed, there were eleven barges, each with a swivel carronade cannon mounted in the bow.

Forty British marines were already on Noddle's Island,

and they were soon joined by one hundred Regulars sent across the harbor by General Gage. The barges, manned by oarsmen, headed for the scene. Each had about thirty marines aboard, all from the various men-of-war anchored in Boston Harbor, with many off the famed vessel *Somerset*,* which had just completed a sortie up and down the New England coast.

The battle now began in earnest with General Putnam in active command of the American forces. The sloop, the schooner and several barges opened fire on the Yankees, under cover of which the British marines began to advance slowly on the Rebels.

Putnam laid his plan of battle. Seeing that the British craft would pass between Hog Island and the Chelsea mainland, he ordered his men to dig themselves into the marsh ditches alongside the creek, and when the enemy came within range the Americans would be in a position to begin a devastating fire. First, however, he would have to meet and engage the 150 marines then at Noddle's Island. The Americans were told not to shoot "until they had opportunity to fire with effect upon the enemy." Thus Putnam adopted a practice which also paid off three weeks later at Bunker Hill.

Advancing slowly in well-drawn-up lines, which made them excellent targets, the British marines came closer and closer. Finally, when the troops were just a few rods from the entrenched Americans, the order to fire was given, and a surprisingly large number of English were killed and wounded. The British now retreated to their barracks at the other end of Noddle's Island.

---

* This craft not only figured in the subsequent Battle of Bunker Hill and is mentioned in Longfellow's "Midnight Ride of Paul Revere," but also was later wrecked at Cape Cod under tragic circumstances.

Having gained the first advantage, the Yankees withdrew across the ford to Hog Island where other American forces were then arriving. Meanwhile the British Regulars from Noddle's Island began firing by platoons across the creek at the fleeing Americans, but they hit very few.

Hastily clearing Hog Island of all cattle and sheep, the Yankees fled across to Chelsea Neck, where they sent out runners for reinforcements.

General Putnam now decided to participate physically in the battle, bringing with him three hundred additional men and two four-pound cannons. This is the very first time the Americans used artillery in battle against the enemy!

The gallant General Joseph Warren, who was destined to die at Bunker Hill, volunteered and joined the American forces. It was not until about nine o'clock in the evening that the Continental forces, now more than a thousand men, were at full strength.

Israel Putnam surveyed the situation carefully. Noddle's Island was heavily occupied by a large body of enemy troops. The schooner *Diana* was firing constantly upon the American forces at Chelsea Neck, the sloop which accompanied her stood ready, while scores of British marines waited on the barges.

Instructing his troops to get the two provincial cannons ready, Putnam decided to act. He went down to the shore, off of which the *Diana* was shooting at his men, and in his usual reckless fashion began to shout across to the schooner. As the vessel was within easy speaking distance, the moment for which Putnam had waited was at hand. He bellowed out to the British marines that they were covered from every point and if they would only surrender they would be given the best of treatment. By this time there were several hundred Americans in the natural marsh trenches, out of sight but ready to fire when Putnam gave the command.

Not realizing this, the British marines were exasperated by Putnam's nerve, and their immediate answer was to fire two cannon shots. These were answered at once by the first cannon shots ever fired by American forces anywhere, which were soon reinforced by bullets from hundreds of rifles. This heavy barrage lasted for several hours, during which time the tide reached its height. A large reinforcement of British marines with two twelve-pounders was sent to Noddle's Island, while the armed sloop moved in close to shore and joined in the battle.

Finally the British forces realized that the Americans were killing too many of their men on the schooner and they stopped firing. Agreeing that discretion was far more important than valor at this point, the survivors decided that if they didn't soon escape from their vessel, they would perish on it. Taking to their boats, the British abandoned the *Diana*, which eventually drifted out with the receding tide to scrape ashore on the Winnisimet ferry ways.

Noticing the drifting craft, Isaac Baldwin led a party of twelve provincial soldiers aboard, where they found rich booty that they sorely needed. They removed from the *Diana* "4 double fortified four-pounders, 12 swivels, chief of her rigging and sail, many clothes, some money, & c., which the sailors and marines left behind."

The sloop continued to fire heavily on the Americans, as they removed these spoils of war to two wagons. Elisha Lettinwell was directed to see that the captured supplies reached Continental Headquarters at Cambridge. As Boston Harbor was entirely under the control of the proud

British Navy, the Americans realized they could not capture the *Diana* but had to destroy her. So they set the
schooner on fire by rolling bundles of hay under her stern
and igniting them. The *Diana* was a mass of flames in a
very short time.

Now Israel Putnam shouted to his men to follow him.
Not satisfied with the casualties which he had inflicted on
the British forces from the shore, he led his troops into
the water to finish their task. Soon up to their waists, the
Americans poured such a terrific fire against those on the
sloop that almost everyone was killed.

Coming to the rescue of the beleaguered craft, the
British aboard the barges attempted to pull her off into
deep water so that the Rebels would not be able to follow.
As the tide was going out fast, they failed at first but
finally succeeded on their fourth attempt and were able
to witness the unusual sight of the British Navy fleeing
from Yankee fighters up to their waists in water and
armed only with rifles.

With the removal of the sloop out into the harbor, the
only vessel now firing was the famed British frigate
Somerset. Her cannon had been busy shooting at the
Americans at Chelsea all during the engagement, and now
she let go a few final scattering shots which ended the
engagement.

The impetuous Putnam had won the Battle of Chelsea
Creek.

The spirited words of an unknown poet follow:

*There the old-fashioned colonel galloped through the white
infernal*
    Powder cloud;

*And his broad sword was swinging, and his brazen throat
was ringing*
> *Trumpet loud;*
> *There the blue bullets flew,*
*And the trooper jackets redden at the touch of the leaden
> Rifle breath;*
*And rounder, rounder, rounder, roared the iron six-pounder,
> Hurling death.*

The reader may wonder why this second battle of the
Revolution had been so universally ignored. Richard
Frothingham in his book *The Siege of Boston* did not
want to give Putnam the credit for being commander at
the Battle of Bunker Hill.* If he had given the Battle of
Chelsea Creek its rightful importance, proclaiming Putnam's triumphantly successful command there, the general's place at the later Battle of Bunker Hill would have
had to have been given more emphasis in history. Therefore the engagement at Chelsea Creek was ignored by the
historian.

Evidence of the fact that Chelsea Creek ** was the real
second battle in our struggle for liberty can be found in
the newspapers of the day. In the pages of the *New
Hampshire Gazette and Chronicle* for June 2, 1775, we
read that at the battle of Chelsea Creek there were between two hundred and three hundred British marines

---

* The battle was not fought at Bunker Hill, but at Breed's Hill.
** Incidentally, those of you who may search for Chelsea Creek today,
will not discover it on any modern map or chart! To facilitate passage
up Chelsea Creek of gigantic oil tankers, one of which could without
effort carry on their decks the entire British fleet participating in this
second battle of the Revolution, the waterway was dredged to a depth
of more than thirty feet. Because of this new depth, Chelsea Creek
became Chelsea River, and is so designated on all modern maps and
charts.

and regulars killed, and that "a Place was dug in Boston
25 feet square to bury their Dead."

Later, in the *Boston Gazette and Country Journal,* for
Monday, June 19, 1775, we find that a gentleman who
left Boston about June 6 stated "for Fact, that he saw
landed on the Long Wharf at that Place, out of one boat
alone, no less than 64 dead men that had been killed by
the Provincials at the late Attack at Noddle's and Hog
Islands, as mentioned in our last."

Any reference to Putnam inevitably brings up the story
of his encounter in a wolf den, which has been a Connecticut legend for two centuries. There have been many
distortions of the tale, and there are those who wish to
discredit the story entirely.

Without question, there did exist a fierce female wolf
in Connecticut at the time, which could always be identified by a paw track with several missing claws.

In the winter which began in 1742, Israel Putnam, then
living on his farm in Connecticut, suffered the loss of
seventy of his sheep and goats in one night. He was
furious, and when he found large wolf tracks in the vicinity with the missing claws on one paw, he recognized the
killer.

Calling together five of his Pomfret neighbors, Putnam
organized a pursuit by having the men take turns hunting
in pairs, with two tracking ahead while four followed
behind. In this manner they had the animal constantly on
the run. They pursued their quarry west until it turned
back toward the scene of the slaughter.

After traveling all night, the six hunters reached a position within three miles of Putnam's Pomfret farmhouse
at ten the next morning. Seventeen-year-old John Sharp,
one of the six men, outstripped the other trackers and

trailed the beast to her den. The other five soon reached the cave, and the news spread rapidly that the wolf was cornered.

That entire day was spent by Putnam and his friends in attempting to smoke out the creature. When a dog was sent into the den the frightened animal came out with terrible lacerations. The other hounds now showed a definite unwillingness for further participation in the affair.

His neighbors now suggested that Putnam send his servant into the den to kill the wolf, but the man was too terrified to be of any use. Putnam then took off his coat and waistcoat, determined to finish the wolf himself.

The cave goes straight back about twenty-five feet into the side of the hill, and is roughly about a yard across at its widest point and not much higher. Putnam tore great sections of birch bark from neighboring trees and improvised a torch from the birch. After tying a long rope around his legs so that he could be pulled out if he signaled that he was in trouble, he told the others that he was ready. Dauntlessly he lighted the torch and started into the cave.

Crawling slowly along over the frozen snow and ice, the general heard ominous growls from the darkness ahead. Soon he was able to detect the fiery eyes of the beast. The wild animal gnashed her teeth and growled, readying herself for the spring she must make to defend herself. Having decided that he had seen enough to go back for his gun, Putnam gave the signal to be pulled out.

His friends, hearing the snarls of the wolf, decided that the general had been attacked and instead of pulling him slowly along, they yanked him out unceremoniously. His shirt was stripped off right over his head and his body was terribly scratched.

Nevertheless, after recovering his breath, Putnam decided that he was going back in with his musket. Loading his famous gun with nine buckshot, he started toward the den, holding his weapon in one hand and his torch in the other, with the lines still tied to his legs. Kneeing his way forward, he finally confronted his prey.

He took careful aim as the wolf tensed herself to spring. Just as the beast was about to leap at him, he fired. The noise in that rock-enclosed vault was deafening, and mingled with the dirt and dust in the cave the smoke from his gun created an impenetrable cloud.

His helpers pulled him out more carefully this time and after waiting for the smoke and dust to clear, Putnam went back into the cave to discover the results of his shot. There was not a sound from the she-wolf as he neared her. Finally he was so close that he touched her nose with his lighted torch. When there was no response he knew that this terror of the farmlands of almost all eastern Connecticut, was dead.

Putnam "grasped her ears, kicked the rope," and again was slowly pulled from the den. His associates cheered when they saw the body of the wolf. The entire party carried the dead animal up over the treacherous icy face of the hill to the Kingsbury Tavern and suspended it from a beam, "into which an iron spike had been driven." At the hour of midnight a celebration was held, attended by every farmer for miles around.

Another notable incident in the life of Israel Putnam occurred in February, 1779, when he was almost trapped by British horsemen. At the time the highway was frozen with snow and ice. Putnam's steed carried him swiftly away from his pursuers, but his mount eventually began to tire. At one side of the road, the general noticed a steep cliff descending into a ravine, and he galloped toward this.

Reaching the edge of the precipice, he urged his horse over the cliff which is now known as Horseneck Height. Down they plunged toward a slender path far below. Again and again the animal almost lost his balance, but each time he recovered his footing, and the ride was accomplished successfully. The British pursuers were dumfounded. Firing several unsuccessful revolver shots, at which Putnam waved his drawn sword, the crestfallen Englishmen returned to their own camp.

On another occasion he had a narrow escape from burning by the Indians. Captured during the French and Indian War by the Caughnawega Indians on August 8, 1758, Putnam was later tied to a tree, where it was planned that he was to be roasted alive. A sudden rain storm put out the fire which the savages had started under him, but the red men rekindled the flames with dry twigs.

Suddenly an ally of the Indians, a French officer named Molang, rushed through the braves and kicked the fire away from the American. Undoing his lashings, Molang freed the prisoner who was escorted to the French fort the next day, and on August 14, under a flag of truce, was taken to Fort Ticonderoga where he was, under pretense of being an "old man," released two months later.

During his declining years his residence became part of Brooklyn, Connecticut, which was incorporated in 1786. Four years later, Israel Putnam died at his farmhouse there on Saturday, May 29, 1790.

The general was buried in a tomb above ground in the

Brooklyn cemetery. A marble slab was placed on top of the grave with an epitaph by Timothy Dwight of Yale. Unfortunately souvenir hunters so mutilated the marble marker that for safety it was removed to the Capitol building at Hartford, Connecticut, where it was placed in the lower corridor, to confuse future generations with the impression that the body lay beneath it.

Nor are the remains of Israel Putnam in the Brooklyn cemetery where he was originally buried. A plot of ground was chosen near the Brooklyn public square, on the northeast corner of the historic Mortlake property. In 1888 Putnam's remains were placed in a sarcophagus built into the foundation of the monument which is topped by an equestrian statue of the famous Revolutionary soldier.

And so it was that the restlessness which characterized his life followed him after death and his body was moved to one part of Connecticut, while his original tombstone was taken many miles distant.

General Putnam was one of the greatest soldiers of the Revolutionary War. Best of all, I like to recall this truly legendary character wading through Chelsea Creek, urging his men on in this forgotten engagement of the American Revolution.

11

THE MANTLE OF DEATH

ALTHOUGH TENS OF THOUSANDS of people walk by a tablet
set into the building at 333 Washington Street, Boston,
few of them notice it. The inscription reads as follows:
Here Stood THE PROVINCE HOUSE/ Occupied by the
Royal Governors/ of the Province of Massachusetts Bay/
until the Evacuation of Boston by/ the British Army
March 17, 1776/ Residence of Peter Sargeant/ Built
1679/ Bought by the Province/ April 11, 1716/ This
Tablet placed by the/ Massachusetts Society/ Sons of the
Revolution/ 1923. That plaque marks the scene of a
tragic drama early in the eighteenth century.

In the year 1679, Peter Sargeant, a wealthy and public-
spirited citizen of Boston, built a handsome residence
for himself in the heart of the Athens of America. It was
a magnificent mansion, the like of which up to that time
had not been seen anywhere else in New England. For his
estate Sargeant chose a location which today is in the very
center of downtown Boston. The property had a frontage

98

of eighty-six feet on what is now Washington Street, and a depth of 266 feet.

Built of Dutch brick which was laid in English bond with clay and shell mortar, the residence had huge timbers and great beams. Not only was it three stories high, but the attic, lighted by dormer windows, was large and spacious. High above the building was a great octagonal lantern cupola, which today might be called a widow's walk. From this great cupola almost every landmark of the entire surrounding countryside could be readily identified. With the use of spyglasses even the outermost islands of Boston Harbor were visible. The view to the north, west and south was equally gratifying.

The front doorway of the mansion was reached by a wide flight of broad red freestone steps fenced in by curiously wrought-iron balustrades. Over the porch was another iron balustrade, in which were worked the date of building and Peter Sargeant's initials: 16 P. S. 79.

High above the town of Boston was a copper statue of an Indian affixed to the top of the cupola, looking down on all traffic along what was then Marlboro Street and Corn Hill. This unusual ornament indeed became a historic landmark, which could be seen on a clear day for miles around Boston town. It was constructed with particular care by Shem Drowne, the same man who designed and built the famous grasshopper atop Faneuil Hall.

When Lord Bellomont * arrived in Boston in 1699 as governor of New England, he was anxious to occupy a residence equal to his importance. Hearing of Bellomont's wishes, Peter Sargeant graciously moved out of

---

* Lord Bellomont was the betrayer of privateer William Kidd.

the stately mansion he had constructed twenty years before and Lord Bellomont moved in at once. Every royal
governor who followed, from Shute to Gage, used this
edifice as his own residence. Peter Sargeant died in 1716,
and the province purchased the great estate for twenty-
three hundred pounds.

The interior of the mansion, which only then became
known as the Province House, was a showplace. The
wide double-entrance door opened into the hall, on the
right of which was a spacious room. It was here that the
ancient governors, surrounded by their councils and leaders, held sway.

Hawthorne, who visited the building in 1850, has left
hints of its former magnificence. He tells us that "the
most venerable ornamental object is a chimney piece set
round with Dutch tiles of blue-figured china, represent-
ing scenes from Scripture."

The great staircase, winding as it did up through the
center of the mansion, was magnificent, with "its broad
steps having each flight terminating in a square landing
place, whence the ascent is continued toward the cupola."
Up these stairs the military boots, or possibly the gouty
shoes of many a governor had trodden as the wearers
mounted to the cupola which afforded them so wide a
view over their metropolis and the surrounding country.
The cupola had an opening upon the roof. From this
vantagepoint Gage may have observed his disastrous victory on Bunker Hill, while Howe probably marked the
approaches of Washington's besieging army.

Hawthorne was deeply impressed with his visit to the
Province House and became so interested in the venerable
edifice that he spent some time there, gathering what tid-
bits he could out of the ancient past. Usually he had the

help of "an elderly person" he had originally met while drinking a glass of port sangaree, prepared by landlord Thomas Waite.

From his visits to the Province House, Hawthorne wrote four stories, including *Howe's Masquerade, Randolph's Portrait* and *Old Esther Dudley.* His fourth tale was the master production of his visits there and has always filled me with a strange horror! This story, *Lady Eleanore's Mantle,* is well founded on fact, but Hawthorne admits "some suitable adornments." Actually, it is fairly easy to reconstruct the background of the story.

Boston, on many occasions in the early days, was visited by the smallpox. It was first prevalent in town in November, 1633, but was not an epidemic. Returning in 1666, the disease caused the death of at least forty persons. In November, 1698, it was extremely fatal in both town and country, and four years later again carried off many inhabitants.

In October, 1716, Colonel Samuel Shute, a grandson of the Puritan divine, Joseph Caryl, became governor, his friends having purchased the office from the king's appointee for one thousand pounds. Arriving on October 4, aboard a merchant ship, Governor Shute was tendered a royal welcome which included a parade to the Province House. Once settled in office, however, he did not get along well with the citizens of Massachusetts, and among other things his term was marred by the worst smallpox epidemic in the entire history of Boston. It was believed to have been brought from a ship which had entered Newport, Rhode Island.

Aboard the vessel was a relative of Governor Shute named Lady Eleanore Rochcliffe who had come to America to live in the Province House. All of her close relatives had died, leaving Samuel Shute her nearest of kin. Hearing of the splendid mansion in which the governor lived, she decided to accept the invitation of his wife and move to New England. Lady Eleanore was a proud and overbearing woman. Combined with a vicious temper, this made her almost impossible to get along with.

She arrived in Boston from Newport in the governor's coach, attended by a small guard of gentlemen on horseback. As the heavy, highly ornamental carriage rumbled through Corn Hill it attracted considerable notice, and the populace had quick glimpses through the large windows of the queenly figure who combined the attitude of a monarch with the beauty and natural grace of a girl in her teens.

Those close enough to notice saw that she wore an embroidered mantle which had been patterned by the best dressmaker in all London a few days before Lady Eleanore had sailed from England. This mantle was of an extremely unusual design and attracted attention wherever she went.

Reaching the governor's mansion, the coachman reined in his four black steeds, and the cavalcade came to a pause in front of the Province House. It was an awkward coincidence that the bell of the Old South Church was just then tolling for a funeral. Captain Langford, an English officer, who had recently brought dispatches to Governor Shute, objected to the bell, but Dr. Clarke, standing nearby, told the courier that even a dead beggar had precedence over a living queen, and explained that "King Death always confers high privileges."

A black-liveried slave leaped from behind the coach and threw open the door. Governor Samuel Shute descended the flight of steps from his mansion to greet his guest. As the governor moved toward the carriage, there was general astonishment when a pale young man, with his black hair all in disorder, rushed from the throng. Prostrating himself beside the coach, he offered his back as a footstool for Lady Eleanore Rochcliffe to tread upon. She held back an instant as if doubting whether the young man were worthy to bear the weight of her foot. But she finally accepted the human step and reached the sidewalk. Taking Governor Shute's arm, she walked majestically up the broad stairs and into the mansion.

The youth who had thus outdone Sir Walter Raleigh went by the improbable name of Jervase Helwyse. Considered a mad, harmless person, Helwyse had fallen violently in love with Lady Eleanore back in England, but she had always ignored him.

Governor Shute soon made arrangements for a gigantic ball to be held at the Province House for his guest. That night four young men in particular had been singly honored by the young Eleanore, looking regal in her mantle, for she had allowed each of them to dance with her. The ambitious Jervase, however, was not among them. Possibly the most outstanding social function in the entire history of the mansion, the ball supplied a topic of conversation for the colonial metropolis many weeks after it took place.

An event which had occurred across the water in England was now to have a devastating effect. About two months previous to the ball a terrible smallpox plague swept that country. One of the first to succumb was the dressmaker who had designed and worked on Lady Eleanore's extraordinary mantle. Some time after the ball, smallpox struck the four young men who had been favored by Lady Eleanore with a dance. The dread disease soon spread to others of the guests, and the socially prominent residents of Boston were taken ill far out of proportion to their numbers. *

Before long all New England was afflicted by the outbreak. It eventually spread to the middle and lower classes and stopped being the exclusive property of the aristocracy. The grip of this epidemic was overwhelming. When the victims died, the contagious dead became enemies of the living. Graves were hastily dug and the victims of pestilence were rapidly interred. Conditions finally became so serious that all Boston's public affairs were transferred to Cambridge.

Each dwelling house into which the scourge entered had a blood-red warning flag that fluttered in the polluted air over the doorway. Hawthorne tells us that such a banner had long waved over the broad portals of the Province House. Then came an awesome discovery. The medical officers of the day proved without question that the epidemic had been brought to Boston through Lady Eleanore's mantle! Its beauty had been conceived in the brain of a woman delirious from the disease, and was the last toil of her dying fingers.

The people of Boston soon began to rave against Lady Eleanore, crying out that her pride and scorn had evoked a fiend and that between them both this monstrous evil had been born. Whenever the red flag was hoisted over another and yet another door, the people clapped their hands and shouted through the streets, in bitter mockery, "A new triumph for the Lady Eleanore!"

And so it was that one day a wild figure approached the Province House. Folding his arms, Jervase Helwyse

---

* Of 6,000 Bostonians who eventually contracted the dread disease, at least 1,000 died.

stood contemplating the scarlet banner which the wind shook fitfully. Climbing one of the pillars by means of the iron balustrade, Jervase took down the flag and entered the mansion, waving the banner above his head. At the foot of the staircase he met Governor Shute, booted and spurred and with his cloak drawn around him, about to leave upon a journey. Stepping past the youth, Governor Shute told him to see the doctor.

The mad man knew that Eleanore was deathly ill from the smallpox, but he wished to visit her in spite of everything.

"Lady Eleanore," called Jervase up the staircase, "Queen of the Plague, I wish to see you seated on the throne with your partner, Death!"

Brushing his way by the doctor, the intruder reached the top of the steps which led to the patient's room, and in anticipation of again viewing her lovely features, he stole to her door.

Pausing on the threshold, Jervase now lost his nerve. He fearfully called into the chamber for Eleanore. There was no answer. He knew he was in the right room for he noticed the dreaded mantle hanging inside the closet door, and there on a table was a beautiful diamond which once had adorned her bosom. In the heavily curtained bed, however, lay a figure of horror. Its sunken features revealed a skeletonlike face, heavily pock-marked, while the body had wasted away to a mere shell.

"What have you done with the Lady Eleanore?" cried Jervase in terror, afraid of the reply.

There came a low moan from the bed.

"My throat is parched. Bring me a drop of water!" The being in the bed stirred slightly, and Jervase fancied that he had heard the voice before.

"Who are you?" cried the lad.

"Oh, Jervase Helwyse," said the voice, and the figure twisted in the bed, as if to hide from the youth her ugliness. "Look not now on that woman whom you once loved. Yes, I am Lady Eleanore. You all have your revenge, for the curse of Heaven has stricken me. I wrapped myself in pride in my mantle, which has now given me this wretched face and body."

Shocked beyond speech, Jervase stared in horror at the apparition of death behind the curtains. Finally he gathered strength enough to shake his finger at the unhappy girl. Beginning to laugh insanely from his shock, he made the very curtains sway in his agitation. Soon the chamber echoed and re-echoed with his disordered merriment.

"Another happy triumph for the Lady Eleanore," screamed the maniac. "All of us were her victims, and who so worthy to be the final victim as Lady Eleanore herself?"

Under the spell of some new thought in his confused mind, Jervase snatched up the fatal mantle of pestilence from its closet hook, after which he rushed out of the chamber. Down the staircase he ran until finally he reached the outer door and disappeared.

Late that night a torchlight procession marched through the streets, with Jervase Helwyse out in front. The effigy of a woman was being pulled through the streets, a woman wearing the embroidered mantle. Winding its way up Summer Street to Marlboro, the parade turned to the right and started down Marlboro Street to Corn Hill. There, directly in front of the Province House, it stopped.

Throwing papers in the street, Jervase and others then tossed faggots on them and put the effigy, still wearing the mantle of death, on top. It was but the work of a moment to light the bonfire, and soon the flames began to consume the pyre. After the fire died down, a strong easterly wind swept in from the sea, scattering away the ashes of the blaze.

From the moment of the complete destruction of the mantle in the flames, the epidemic of smallpox began to falter in its ruthless sweep. A few weeks later it was but a terrible memory.

The Lady Eleanore had passed away the very night of the torchlight procession. Nevertheless, there are those who have believed that her ghost still lurked within the walls of the old Province House until the remains of the edifice were utterly destroyed not many years ago. Even today, in the new Province Building, it is said that a weird female form may sometimes be seen, "shrinking into the darkest corner and muffling her face within an embroidered mantle." If the legend is true, this form can be no other than the once-proud Lady Eleanore.

NEW ENGLAND MERMAIDS
AND MERMEN

STORIES OF NEW ENGLAND mermaids and mermen are few and far between. The first mention of a North American mermaid came in 1610, when a mariner, Captain Whitbourne, reported sighting one in the harbor of Saint John's, Newfoundland, and described the creature with careful delineation.

Four years later, in 1614, during the same voyage when he discovered Monhegan Island off the coast of Maine, Captain John Smith saw a mermaid "swimming about with all possible grace." He pictured her as having large eyes, a finely shaped nose which was "somewhat short," and "well-formed ears" which were rather too long. Smith goes on to say that her "long green hair imparted to her an original character by no means unattractive." He states that he had already begun "to experience the first effects

of love" toward the creature until she revealed that from
the waist down she was in reality a fish.

In 1673 another visitor to America, John Jocelyn, reported that a friend of his, a Mr. Miller, had sighted a
male of the species in Maine's Casco Bay. Miller was out
in his canoe one day when the monster put a hand up
over the side of the canoe and threatened to capsize it.
To save himself, the terrified canoeist seized a hatchet and
chopped off the hand, whereupon the denizen of the
deep sank to the bottom, dyeing the water purple with its
blood, and was seen no more.

Some years later a Gloucester fisherman told of a mermaid who boarded his fishing craft during a calm spell.
Panicked, the sailors attacked the creature with a hatchet.
The mermaid managed to clamber over the side and into
the water, clinging to the taffrail with one hand. Then,
as Miller had done, the frightened fishermen amputated
the hand, and the mermaid sank immediately. She came
to the surface once more and gave a deep human sigh, as
though she felt great pain, and then she disappeared for
good. Later when the men examined the hand they
found it had five fingers with fingernails exactly like those
of a woman.

Early in the eighteenth century, another mermaid was
said to have been sighted off Nantucket Island from a
passing vessel. It is unfortunate that the details of this
encounter are lacking, for the creature is reported to have
swum ashore and disappeared into the strange forest at
Great Point. Over two centuries later a Great Point lighthouse keeper found evidence that someone had lived in
the forest, and some believe it may have been a mermaid
lair.

On May 1, 1714, a traveler and writer named Valentyn,

while on a long voyage, also sighted a creature who may have been the so-called Nantucket Mermaid. I quote from the preacher's pen:

"I, the captain, purser and mate of the watch, and a great many of the ship's company, saw at about the distance of thrice the length of the ship from us, very distinctly, on the surface of the water seemingly sitting with his back to us and half the body above the water, a creature of a grizzlish, or gray color, like that of a codfish skin.

"It appeared like a sailor, or a man sitting on something; and more like a sailor, as on its head there appeared to be something like an English cap of the same color.

"We all agreed that he must be some shipwrecked person. After some time I begged the captain to steer the ship more directly toward it, being somewhat on the starboard side, and we had got within a ship's length of him, when the people on the forecastle made such a noise that he plunged down, head foremost, and got presently out of sight.

"But the man who was on the watch at the masthead declared that he saw him for the space of two hundred yards, and that he had a monstrous long tail."

Evidently bothered by scoffers, in later years Mr. Valentyn made a statement to the effect that if "there shall be found those who disbelieve the existence of such creatures as seamen, or mermaids, of which we have given great reason to believe that there are, let them please themselves: I shall give myself no more trouble about them."

For several generations after this, New England went without local reports concerning mermaids. Then, in the year 1822, a vessel sailed into Boston Harbor commanded by a Captain Dodge who announced that he had not only seen but also captured a mermaid. He declared that he had put her ashore on an island where he planned to educate her in human ways, but he brought back a sketch of the creature with him. After studying his drawing, there were those who told the captain to his face that it had been made from imagination, but the mariner vigorously denied this and warned the skeptics that time would prove the honesty of his claim.

Leaving Boston some days later, Captain Dodge promised to have the mermaid aboard his vessel when he returned. But when he came back several months later he was still without his prize. While his cargo was being unloaded at India Wharf the other sea captains taunted him for his failure to have the sea maid with him. Provoked by their ridicule, Dodge announced that the mermaid had died because he had taken her from her natural home in the ocean. He admitted that her death was his fault and he seemed genuinely remorseful, refusing to discuss the matter further.

A year later, however, when he returned from another voyage the captain was approached by several scientists who had heard about the mermaid. They explained to him that their interest was purely academic and that they were willing to consider the evidence of his having captured a mermaid with an open mind. They sympathized with his remorse over her death but urged him nevertheless to bring the remains back to Boston with him on a future voyage for the purpose of scientific research. Captain Dodge listened to them with respectful attention, but did not give them a definite answer before he again sailed away.

By this time the news that the story of Captain Dodge's mermaid had attracted the interest of scientists had reached the ears of Bostonians in general. Newspapers and periodicals were soon calling the notice of their readers to mermaids. This was done warily at first, but later many local New England editors and writers indulged in general dissertations on the subject. Because of this stimulated interest a few Bostonians and several other New Englanders made it a point to find out just how much had ever been discovered about mermaids. In this research some of them hoped that they would be able to evaluate Captain Dodge's story.

Many of these investigators were pleasantly surprised to discover from their research that mermaids had been reported all over the world almost from the earliest days of antiquity. Even omitting the obvious hoaxes and inaccurate legends which could not be authenticated in any way, they found over a hundred accounts of mermaids. Of that number we shall mention a few outstanding examples.

Both Pliny and Pausanius record instances in which mermaids were sighted, especially around the island of Taprobane, and on the nearby mainland.

Alexander ab Alexandro tells us that Theodore Gaza once saw a mermaid cast ashore in the Morea immediately after a heavy gale had swept the area. Gaza describes this mermaid as having a "human and charming countenance," but with a scaly body and tail. Gaza went on to say that as a crowd gathered on the shore the mermaid became embarrassed and then burst into tears of fright when people pressed too close. Finally, when an opening in the ring of spectators appeared, the mermaid flipped down toward the beach like an inchworm, and disappeared in the raging surf.

In 1403, during a series of great storms, the Holland

dikes broke through. A "sea woman" was driven through the breach into the Parmer Sea where she was caught by the Dutch people. They brought the captive to Edam, where the natives dried her, cleaned "marine impurities" from her and dressed her in clothes. The people at Haarlem heard about the mermaid and she was taken there, where she was taught to eat civilized food and spin yarn. Finally she accepted religion and on her death was given a Christian burial.

In 1554, Fondelet tells of a Polish mermaid clothed by nature "with the garb of a bishop." Then we have the devil mermaid, *monstrum marinum daemoniforme,* captured at Illyria and taken to Antwerp.

It was also found that when King Roger reigned over Sicily, a young man bathing on shore met a mermaid of "great beauty," who remained with him for some time, but never spoke. Finally she returned to the sea and was not seen again.

In 1712 a sea woman was taken alive near the island of Boro. She was fifty-nine inches tall. Refusing to associate with the natives on the island, the mermaid would not eat when offered food, and slowly wasted away. She died after four days and seven hours without uttering a sound. Her remains were preserved by Samuel Falvers in Amboina and were on exhibition for many years. The head was as perfectly proportioned as any female human head could be. The eyes were very light blue, just a little too light to be human. The hair was sea green. She had long arms, hands and breasts, and her upper body was almost as white as that of a woman. The lower part of her body was like the "hinder part of a fish."

In dignified Boston these stories soon became well known as they were repeated from person to person. The arguments for and against the existence of mermaids were thoroughly discussed, but no one dreamed that a mermaid would make a physical appearance in New England.

And so it was that Captain Dodge and his ship appeared one day off Boston Light. The pilot who went aboard knew the captain, and happened to mention the mermaid to the mariner.

"Mermaid?" replied Captain Dodge. "I've got her aboard!"

"A joke is a joke, captain," said the pilot. "Surely you are not serious."

"That I am, sir, for I have her incased in a transparent coffin. Just you wait until we get the cargo unloaded."

And that was all the pilot could learn. Of course, as soon as the vessel docked the news was flashed up and down the waterfront that Captain Dodge had really brought the mermaid back with him.

Within a week the lifeless remains of the creature in a glass case were on public exhibition where they attracted widespread attention. Many scientists and laymen alike wished to remove the glass and examine the remains more closely but Captain Dodge was firm. He would not allow it. He had brought the mermaid to Boston to prove he had not exaggerated, but all must view her at a respectful distance.

The greatest showman of them all, Phineas T. Barnum, naturally had to produce the mummified remains of another mermaid to satisfy his audiences, but there are those who said that this particular exhibit was presented with tongue in cheek.

On October 31, 1881, many of those who had viewed the remains of Captain Dodge's mermaid more than a half century before were interested in the announcement that a mermaid had been "captured in Aspinwall Bay. Her head and body were very plainly and distinctly marked as that of a woman. The face, eyes, nose, mouth, teeth, arms, breasts and hair were unquestionably human. The hair was a pale, silky blonde, several inches in length. The arms terminated in claws closely resembling an eagle's talons, instead of fingers with nails. From the waist up, the resemblance to a woman is perfect, and from the waist down, the body is exactly the same as the ordinary mullet of our waters, with its scales, fins and tail perfect. Many old fishermen and amateur anglers who have seen it pronounce it unlike any fish they have ever seen. Scientists and savants alike are all at sea respecting it, and say that if the mermaid be indeed a fabulous creature, they cannot class this strange comer from the blue waters."

While many of the viewers of Captain Dodge's exhibit were convinced that they were staring at the dead body of an actual mermaid, the majority of visitors to the glass coffin scoffed at what they saw. The more scientific witnesses were of the opinion that the exhibit consisted of the upper part of a human torso, carefully joined around the hips to the lower body and tail of a fish. No matter what they believed, however, those who saw this exhibit were frequently called upon for the remainder of their lives to recount how a mermaid had appeared in Boston.

When Captain Dodge concluded his exhibition and took his attraction away, he returned to his first love, the sea, but nobody knows what happened to the girl-fish in the glass coffin.

Let us allow the newspapers of the period, whose editors were just as divided in their opinions as their readers,

to close this chapter with their comments made at the
time about Captain Dodge's exhibit.

CONCORD GAZETTE: *IMPOSITION!*

THE STATESMEN: *A dried old maid.*

BOSTON GAZETTE: *This is a mermaid.*

WAMPOA, CHIEFTAIN OF THE MASSACHUSETTS

Every weekday of the year, as part of their morning motorized chariot race toward Boston, Massachusetts, thousands of autoists cross the bridge which spans Black's Creek between Merrymount and the Wollaston Boulevard.

Many of these drivers may glance over at Treasure Island, located across the highway from the beach itself. It is a fine combination parking area and playground with many outdoor facilities. Should we turn back the pages of Greater Boston history to the pre-Pilgrim era, we would find a short distance away another island attracting the attention of the nearby residents. This was Halfmoon Island, a short way out to sea from the Black's Creek area.

Four hundred years ago, before the great plague spoken of by explorer Dermer decimated Indian life in the vicinity, Halfmoon Island was the red man's pleasure resort. As late as 1689 it was a veritable fairyland of about ten acres. A century before when the Indians were active, it was probably much larger. Gracefully proportioned in the shape of a quarter-, rather than a half-moon, it abounded in wild turkey, quail and pheasant which could be shot with bow and arrow. Blueberries and strawberries were enjoyed in season. The surrounding flats yielded the most succulent clams and lobsters which were easily caught. At high tide sea bass, codfish and flounders readily allowed themselves to be taken by the Indian fishhooks. During the hunting season scores of Indian canoes were drawn up at Halfmoon Island, and when the evening festivities were at their height giant bonfires could be seen for miles around. In time, however, the plague and the relentless encroachment of the white man reduced the numbers of the redskin.

One of the first white followers of the Indian custom of enjoying the insular pleasures of Halfmoon Island was a lad named John Quincy born in 1689. Quincy grew up to become one of the leading citizens of the South Shore of Massachusetts. Graduating from Harvard with the class of 1708, he was soon chosen to represent the Braintree area in the General Court, filling that post for 28 years, and he was Speaker of the House from 1729 to 1741.

When he was growing up, Quincy often visited Halfmoon Island to hunt and fish. Later, when he was a leading Massachusetts citizen and had built his own fine residence on Mount Wollaston, he would often sail up to Boston on his sloop, leaving it at Long Wharf. On the last day of the legislative week, it was his custom to invite his friends aboard the boat, cast off from Long Wharf, and sail with them down to a point off Halfmoon Island.

There he would send his faithful retainer ashore to prepare a clambake and pick any berries which happened to be in season.

Meanwhile, the sloop would draw up at the Quincy pier and discharge its passengers, who were taken across to the mansion, given their rooms for the weekend and told to change into their outing garments for the trip to Halfmoon Island. Soon all would be ready and back aboard the sloop they would go for what Charles Francis Adams later called "strawberry parties."

Colonel John Quincy died in 1767, the same year that John Quincy Adams was born. Indeed, for a brief period it appeared that the Quincy name would vanish from the area, but in 1792 the present city of Quincy, Massachusetts, was named in John Quincy's honor.

Many years before the landing of the white men, there lived on the South Shore of Massachusetts, in sight of Halfmoon Island, a young Neponset Indian named Wampoa. His comrades of the Neponset tribe had recently declared war with their neighbors, the Naticks, and deadly hostilities soon began.

It was noticed, however, that although Wampoa was considered brave and strong, he did not enter into the active fighting, "loitering behind, joining neither the toil of war nor the victory dance."

Wampoa loved to go into the forests to hunt game, and he almost always returned with deer and rabbits which his arrows had brought down. His tribesmen suspected, however, that there must be some more pressing reason than his love of hunting that kept him from joining in the struggles which the Neponset Indians were having with the Naticks. And they were right.

One bright sunny morning in early spring, when Wampoa took his bow and arrows and left his clay cabin on the shores of Boston Harbor to paddle away in his sturdy canoe, several of his comrades in the Neponset tribe secretly followed him. Two hours later, far up the Neponset River, Wampoa paddled ashore in the very center of a primeval forest. Pulling his canoe into a secluded glen, he buckled his sharp hunting knife to his side and took his bow and arrows from the canoe. Then he strode from the glen deep into the heavy growth of forest.

Walking silently for some time, Wampoa finally arrived at a small clearing in the very heart of the woods. Pausing, he gave an imitation of the song of a thrush, after which he waited quietly. Then in the distance he heard an answering whistle.

A minute or two later a young Indian girl stepped from the shadows of the trees, her costume indicating that she was of high birth in the rival Natick tribe. Her primitive dress, according to an ancient chronicle, "served to conceal a form of even more perfect symmetry than is our lot to encounter in the walks of civilization." Her name was Marremette, and she was the daughter of Chief Conestoga.

Meanwhile, back on the shore, Wampoa's tribesmen had discovered his canoe hidden in the foliage, and they were tracking him through the thick forest. Reaching the small clearing, they found the two lovers together and then withdrew, returning to the village of the Neponset with their evidence.

That night, when Wampoa returned, he had with him in his canoe three fine deer as proof of his hunting prowess, but his fellow braves were awaiting him for another reason. His chief questioned Wampoa about the meeting with Marramette in the forest.

The young lover, chagrined at first that he had been detected, soon freely admitted his affection for the girl, and declared with vehemence that he would never give her up. When he saw his arguments were futile, the chief decided to drop the matter for the time being.

Nor were Marramette's visits to the forest unobserved by members of her own tribe. The following week a party of Naticks, which included the young Onamatchee, a brave who had applied for and received the hand of Marramette from her father, sighted the girl deep in the forest. At the time she was making her way to the meeting place. Her betrothed left his companions and followed his bride-to-be alone through the underbrush. He watched as the two lovers met. In great anger he raised his bow and arrow to shoot Wampoa. The form of Marramette interfered, however, and Onamatchee finally withdrew and returned to his party, where he told them of the presence of one of the hated Neponsets.

Silently the Natick warriors deployed around the meeting place of the two lovers. Suddenly, even though Wampoa had not heard the slightest sound, he sensed that all was not well. Springing to his feet, he tightened his belt where were secured his knife and tomahawk. Then he threw the loop of his bow string over the yielding yew, and was ready for trouble.

Within a minute twenty members of the Natick tribe, including Onamatchee himself, stepped out of the forest to form a circle around the Neponset brave. Wampoa sprang backward into the woods, where he scrambled up over a giant rock, and sliding quickly down on the other side, he escaped.

A remarkable runner, he soon outdistanced his pursuers. Then he lay in wait for them. As they came up he killed them one by one from his ambush until seven Naticks lay dead at his feet. Then he was overwhelmed by the surviving members of the tribe and taken back through the forest to their chief.

Chief Conestoga, the father of Marramette, quickly decreed that Wampoa should receive torture by fire until death. The Natick braves then took him to the place of punishment, on the banks of the Neponset River, where they began preparing heaps of dry branches and sticks for the ordeal.

Wampoa, who already had been terribly tortured, saw that his only chance was to feign exhaustion. In his apparently weakened condition he was more or less ignored by the others who were preoccupied with the preparation of the pyre. Quietly he worked his fingers and wrists back and forth to loosen the rawhide thongs that bound him. Then in a tremendous effort, he burst his bonds and found himself free.

Wampoa now watched his chance. At last, when most of the braves were some distance away he came to life in a flash, bounding erect with a powerful spring. Throwing down his rawhide thongs he began to run like the wind, and before the startled Natick warriors knew what was taking place, Wampoa had reached the banks of the Neponset River. Plunging into the stream, he swam under water for almost a hundred feet. Coming up briefly to fill his lungs, he disappeared below the surface again almost before he was sighted.

Reaching the opposite shore far down the river, the fugitive clambered up the bank, and ran rapidly into the underbrush. Knowing that he would be followed, he doubled back toward the river, coming out a quarter mile be-

low. Then he slipped quietly into the Neponset again,
and was soon a mile down the stream.

All the time that he had been in sight the outraged
Naticks were shooting their arrows at him, but not one hit
its mark. Nevertheless, to five of the Naticks it became a
point of honor to catch this hated member of the rival
tribe.

Wampoa was equally determined to get revenge for his
capture and torture. Reaching the point on the river
where he had secreted his trusty canoe, he pulled it from
the underbrush. After he carried it to the bank, he began
to paddle downstream. Meanwhile the five Natick warriors were following in two canoes.

Wampoa planned that he would lure his pursuers out
to Halfmoon Island where he could kill them one by one.
Aiding his plan, the midnight moon now came out from
behind broken clouds. Wampoa paddled rapidly toward
the open sea. His craft was so lightly made that he could
keep the Naticks in their heavier war canoes from gaining
rapidly. His plan was to reach Halfmoon Island just a
little ahead of the first pursuer. The tide was now almost
dead low.

An hour later he pulled his craft ashore on the flats of
Halfmoon Island. Reaching the harder ground, he shoul-
dered his canoe and carried it toward the grove of trees
on the island. Leaving his craft against the first tree in
easy sight of his followers, he started to carry out the
final step of his scheme.

Crouching down behind the ridge of gravel which led
toward what is now Black's Creek, he moved quickly. He
stayed low enough to be unobserved by those in the oncoming first canoe. When he reached a point a quarter
mile from the place where he had put his own craft, Wam-

poa gouged out the sand on the ridge and prepared a perfect ambush.

Paddling desperately, the Indians in the first canoe reached the Halfmoon flats. Now that they were within reach of his arrows, Wampoa took careful aim at the bow paddler. He sent his quiver deep into the body of the first Indian, killing him at once. Having no idea whence the arrow came, the other paddler was an easy victim for the second shot.

Wampoa sprang up at once, raced toward the Natick canoe, jumped in, and paddled it around in the deep water to the other side of the island which faced what is now Adams Shore. Pulling it high on the beach, he walked through the clam flats back to Halfmoon Island, where he awaited the arrival of the second group of pursuing Naticks.

In the second craft were three Indian braves, but from the moment they sighted Halfmoon Island they didn't have a chance. One by one Wampoa's arrows picked them off, leaving him alone in his triumph.

With the turning of the tide Wampoa loaded the five bodies into one canoe. Tying it securely to his own craft, he started paddling back toward the land of the Naticks. By now the moon had set. He paddled slowly, allowing the tide to help him until daylight came. Then he hid under overhanging branches all that day until the following night, when he continued upstream.

Reaching a point in the river opposite the camp of the hostile redmen, he cut the lashes of the second canoe, pushing it ashore near several other canoes of the Natick tribe, where the gruesome cargo was sure to be seen when daylight came.

Paddling farther upstream, he went ashore and pulled

his canoe out of sight under the trees. There he awaited developments, climbing the highest tree and looking down toward the hostile camp.

With the coming of morning the canoe with their five dead tribesmen was found by the Naticks and there was great excitement. Wampoa was considered some sort of demon, and his enemies determined not to pursue him again.

There was one man, however, who decided to act, but not against Wampoa. Onamatchee realized that if he wanted his betrothed, he would have to take matters into his own hands. With one of his warrior friends he called on Conestoga, whom they seized and bound, after which they carried him into the woods. The braves went to the wigwam of Marramette and forcibly removed her. Finally, in possession of both Marramette and her father, Onamatchee declared he would kill the chief in sight of his daughter if she would not marry him.

Onamatchee, however, had made his plans without taking Wampoa into consideration. At the first sign of trouble the Neponset warrior scrambled down from his lookout post atop the high tree and hurried into the forest, where he soon reached the clearing.

He arrived just as Marramette was pleading for the life of her father and Onamatchee was explaining that only if she became his bride would he spare Conestoga. This she refused to do, and finally the brave raised his tomahawk to strike. Placing his foot on the bosom of the older man, he was about to bring the weapon down, but a swifter hand than his took over. Leaping into the fray, Wampoa crashed his tomahawk into Onamatchee's skull, killing him instantly. A second Natick Indian seized his own knife and buried it in the body of Marramette's father, but was instantly slain by Wampoa a second later.

In this tragic manner Wampoa and Marramette found the way finally clear for their marriage. After tenderly carrying the remains of Conestoga into the canoe, Wampoa took his grieving bride-to-be to the bow of the craft. The tide had turned and was now ebbing as the two lovers silently paddled downstream and across to Half-moon Island, where the body of Conestoga was buried.

In due time Wampoa became Chief of the Massachusetts, a tribe which grew in strength until the terrible pestilence swept New England a few years before the Pilgrims landed at Plymouth.

Today, not only are all the pure-blooded Indians gone from the Boston Harbor and Massachusetts area, but Half-moon Island, where Wampoa and Marramette spent their Indian honeymoon, has also vanished.

14

HANGING THE WRONG MAN
ON PURPOSE

THE GOOD PEOPLE WHO NOW reside in North Weymouth, Massachusetts, are particularly fortunate in having as part of their community the Wessagusset Yacht Club, which is located at the base of a hill on the shores of Boston Harbor. The name Wessagusset goes back to earliest times in New England, and was remembered for many years because of a legend which is unparalleled in Massachusetts history.

Thomas Weston of London was extremely anxious to set up a trading post not far from the colony which the Pilgrims had established in 1620. Actually a commercial trader who believed there was a great opportunity in the New World, he hadn't the slightest interest in any of the principles for which the Pilgrims stood.

In the month of May, 1622, ten men arrived at Boston Harbor in an open boat. Originally sent out from London by Weston, they had gone ashore at many of the islands along the New England coast as they approached Boston Harbor. Then, skirting the area which now includes Boston and Quincy, they proceeded south of Fore River to start a settlement where the Wessagusset Yacht Club stands today. The colony, composed of halfhearted workers, did not prosper.

Meanwhile Weston was sending sixty other adventurers across the ocean aboard two small craft, the *Charity* and the *Swan*. Landing at Plymouth late in June, 1622, these "rude fellows" caused great excitement and trouble. To the obvious relief of the Pilgrims, they started for Boston Harbor from Plymouth in the middle of August and finally reached Wessagusset. There they became involved in difficulty after difficulty, and the following winter a goodly number of them died from starvation and sickness.

When supplies ran low at the settlement, a young London boy visited the camp of nearby Indians. As the red men were absent, he stole a substantial amount of corn. His footprints were traced by the savages back to the white men's colony, and a group of braves went to Wessagusset to demand satisfaction.

"We wish you to give the thief English justice," one of the Indians shouted. "You hang Indians when they steal; now you must hang whites for stealing from the Indians."

The members of the Weston community then held a hurried conference, and a spokesman named Will Sommers suggested a solution. An old man who had been a weaver now lay sick in bed. It was Sommers' idea that the invalid be dressed in the real culprit's clothes and hanged in his place so that the younger, more useful member of the group should live, and the colonists agreed. So it was that the protesting weaver was taken from his sick bed, hurriedly arrayed in the garments of the guilty boy, gagged, tied securely and brought out to be sacrificed for the younger man. In front of a gallows hastily erected on the site of what is now the Wessagusset Yacht Club property, and in the presence of all the white men of the settlement as well as the entire Indian tribe, the innocent victim was hanged for a crime which he did not commit. The Indians then went home satisfied that a white man had atoned for his crime against them, and they never found out about the cruel substitution.

Thomas Morton of Merrymount fame, who was liked neither by Pilgrim nor Puritan, wrote of the hanging in his *New English Canaan*. In disrepute because of his Maypole dances with the Indian girls, Morton seized on the incident to get revenge for his being deported from the area. Excerpts from his writings follow:

"Master Weston's plantation being settled at Wessaguscus, his servants, or many of them, being lazy persons that would use no endeavor to take the benefit of the country, some of them fell sick and died.

"One among the rest, an able-bodied man that ranged the forest to see what it would afford him, stumbled by accident on an Indian granary, concealed, as the custom was with those people, underground; and from it he took a capful of corn, and then went his way. The Indian owner, finding by the footprint that the thief was an Englishman, came and made his complaint at the plantation.

"The chief commander of the company immediately called together a parliament of all those who were not sick, to hear and determine the cause of complaint. And wisely now, they should consult upon this huge complaint, that a knife or a string of beads would well enough have disposed

of, Edward Johnson being made a special judge of this
business.

"The fact was there in repetition, construction made that
it was a felony, and by the laws of England punished with
death; and this in execution must be put for an example,
and likewise to appease the savage; when straightway one
arose, moved as it were with some compassion, and said
he could not well gainsay the former sentence, yet he had
conceived within the compass of his brain an Embrion that
was of special consequence to be delivered and cherished.
He said that it would most aptly serve to pacify the savage's complaint, and save the life of one that might (if
need should be) stand them in some good stead, being
young and strong, fit for resistance against an enemy, which
might come unexpected for anything they knew.

"This oration was liked by every one; and the orator was
entreated to show how this end might be reached. He went
on:

"Says he, 'You all agree that one must die, and one shall
die. This young man's clothes we will take off, and put
upon one that is old and impotent,—a sickly person that
cannot escape death; such is the disease on him confirmed,
that die he must; put the young man's clothes on this man,
and let the sick person be hanged in the others stead.'
'Amen,' says one; and so say many more."

Thirty years later, a poet named Butler, in a poem
called "Hudibras," tells of the hanging as follows:

> Though nice and dark the point appear,
> Quoth Ralph, it may hold up and clear.
> That sinners may supply the place
> Of suffering saints, is a plain case.
> Justice give sentence many times
> On one man for another's crimes.
> Our brethren of New England use

Choice malefactors to excuse,
And hang the guiltless in their stead,
Of whom the churches have less need.
As lately 't happened; in a town
There liv'd a cobbler, and but one
That out of doctrine could cut use,
And mend men's lives as well as shoes.
This precious brother having slain,
In time of peace, an Indian,
Not out of malice, but mere zeal,
Because he was an infidel,
The mighty Tottipottimoy
Sent to our elders an envoy,
Complaining sorely of the breach
Of league, held forth by brother Patch,
Against the articles in force
Between both churches, his and ours.
But they maturely having weigh'd
They had no more but him o' th' trade,
A man that serv'd them in a double
Capacity to teach and cobble,
Resolv'd to spare him; yet to do
The Indian Hoghan Moghan too
Impartial justice, in his stead did
Hang an old weaver that was bedrid.

Governor William Bradford, in his *Of Plimoth Planta-tion,* comments briefly on the affair: *"Yea, in ye end they were faine to hange one of their men . . . to give ye Inde-ans contente."*

THRENODIA

THE FIRST SCITUATE, Massachusetts, shipwreck of importance about which we have fairly accurate information
occurred in 1693. Anthony Collamer, or Collamore, left
Scituate Harbor on December 16 of that year, with five
others and a heavy load of wood in his shallop. All were
lost in a gale when the craft hit a boulder now known as
Collamore's Ledge. Collamore's grave, a double stone,
can be found in the Old Meeting House Lane Cemetery
in Scituate about ninety yards east of the site of the
church.

The source of information about this tragedy is a long
poem of twenty-seven stanzas, each stanza running six
lines, entitled "Threnodia." It was written in January,
1694, the year following the wreck, by the Reverend Deodate Lawson of the Second Parish Church in Scituate,
who devoted so much of his time away from the parish,
writing poems of shipwrecks along the shore and preach-
ing at the Salem witch trials, that he was expelled by the

elders in favor of "a pastor more spiritually and more
fixedly disposed."

His "Threnodia" is one of the first American ballads
about the sea and is an example of the best of the early
broadsides in this country. A photograph of the entire
broadside is reproduced elsewhere in this volume, but
the reader will get a picture of the tragedy from the excerpts below:

THRENODIA

*Or a Mournful Remembrance, of the Much to Be
Lamented Death of the Worthy and Pious*

CAPTAIN ANTHONY COLLAMORE

The Great Jehovah is the Lord and King
Both in the Heav'ns and on the Earth and Sea
What things Pleas Him in each to pass doth bring
Nor can he in His Will resisted be.

> He in His Fist retaines the Boistrous Winds
> And raging Waters in a Garment binds

December last upon the Sixteenth day
Within the Harbour lay at Scituate
Some Laden Boats to Boston bound away
Which for Fair Wind and Weather there did wait

> Amongst the Rest was Captain Collamore
> Whose sad disaster, we must now Deplore.

Some Boats with Sailes Expanded Led the way
Out of the Harbour; and did fairly glide;
Thus one by one stood out into the Bay,
With Wind at East North East and Flowing Tide

> The Captain in the Rere did Hoise up Saile,
> And hasted after with a steddy Gale.

He did his best with speed to quit the Shore
And seemed in his way to Prosper well;
He Lufft up to the Wind and North ward bore,
For near an Hour as Spectators tell:

That so he might be gaining of the Wind,
And to his Port the fairer Passage find.

But Dangers great did quickly him surprize
The Clouds did gather and obscure the Sun
Winds Whistled, Snow came thick and Seas did rise;
And He was at a loss which way to run.

As did appear to some that were before,
Who quickly after, saw the Boat no more.

With him Five Persons more Embarqued were
Two Men, one Woman, and two Ladds beside
None did survive alive on Shore appear
But were all Drowned in the ocean wide

No more but two are yet to this day found
Which doth the Hearts of their Relations wound.

Whether some hidden Rock with fatal stroke,
At once gave Final stop unto their Course;
Or whether Laden over deep with Wood,
The Swelling Waves did fill her by degrees;
If then their Frozen Pump would do no good,
They soon became a Prey of o' the Seas;

Which Violently over them did go,
And bore them down, into the deeps below.

One Ephraim Turner near the Fatal place
Was cast upon the Shore and next day found;
Most sorely batter'd on his Head and Face,
Who decently was laid into the ground.

Relations of the Rest did search the Shore,
For thirteen days but they could find no more.

But on the fourteenth day one did espie,
A Corps he judg'd was Captain Collamore
Yet could not know for a Certainty
By anything, but to the Cloathes he wore.

His Form and Visage utterly was lost,
Having by Waves on Rocks been so long toss'd.

Too old and Young this Awfull Sudden Stroke
Doth Testify with loudest Vehemence;
God trys by others Death us to Provoke
While it is Day to work with diligence

Let them both High and Low, rich and poor
Lament the Death of Captain Collamore.

Gemebundus Composuit
Deodate Lawson

A MILLION DOLLAR GAMBLE

THE STRANDING OF THE 441-foot, 7,000-ton Italian craft, *Etrusco*, which occurred during the Saint Patrick's Eve blizzard of 1956, created such an unusual opportunity for the average person to visit a shipwreck at Cedar Point, Scituate, that all records for what might be called maritime audience participation in New England were broken, and more than a million persons went to the site to see the freighter which was destined to become the subject of a new legend of the New England coast. In my previous volume, *The Vengeful Sea*, I recounted the early circumstances of her ill fortune, but now the entire story can be told.

The *Etrusco* was originally built in British Columbia in 1942 as a Canadian Liberty ship. On this fateful voyage in 1956, she sailed from Emden, Germany, in ballast, under the first command of Italian Captain Gaetano Traini. She stopped at the Azores to leave a sick member of the crew, and then continued her journey to arrive in Massachusetts Bay just as the storm broke. Driven by the terrific gale, the vessel was thrown ashore at Cedar Point, also known as Lighthouse Point, in Scituate.

The lights of the freighter were first seen by Charles P. Howland at his residence a short distance from the old Scituate Lighthouse. Both he and Mrs. Howland were startled by the appearance of the craft and amazed at its size, for according to Mrs. Howland, "the ship seemed as big as the *Queen Mary*." She called up the Coast Guard station in Scituate and reported that a vessel was ashore.

Rescue apparatus in charge of Boatswain William E. Miller was despatched to Cedar Point. Meanwhile William A. Rich, BM, AN, in charge of the Point Allerton Coast Guard station, set out for the wreck with ten men and more equipment, while other groups of Coast Guardsmen were ordered to their assistance.

Arriving at the scene, Boatswain Miller soon realized the potential danger of the situation. At its height, the blizzard was striking the area with an 83-mile-an-hour wind, and the snow drifts in the vicinity were piling up nine feet high.

The wind had that ominous high velocity shriek of a great hurricane, heard rarely in the average lifetime. The pelting sand and driving snow was then hitting almost horizontally. The Coast Guardsmen with rescue equipment forced their way through the blinding blizzard, fighting drifts and splashing through flooded areas until they reached the scene of the wreck. There they attempted to shoot lines out over the *Etrusco*. By this time the ship had bumped, thudded and scraped its way over the treacherous, gigantic boulders until it was pushed by wind and waves from its first reported location of nine hundred feet offshore to a position just short of the average high-tide mark.

Boatswain Miller, concerned with the fate of the thirty Italian crewmen on the *Etrusco,* conferred with his men in the parlor of former Selectman and Mrs. James Turner, in charge of the old Scituate Point Lighthouse. As the ship was in very shallow water, and the darkness, high surf and strong, snow-laden winds made rescue by breeches buoy extremely hazardous, it was deemed advisable to wait until daylight before making an attempt. The great bulk of the vessel offered more security at the time than the breeches buoy, provided the ship did not begin to break up under the merciless waves.

At dawn Coast Guardsman Ralph J. Keller of Point Allerton fired the shoulder gun that sent the shot line aboard the ill-fated freighter. The difficult breeches buoy rescue was then carried off smoothly with no casualties.

The crew of the *Etrusco,* as well as scores of other people including myself, will always be grateful to Mrs. Lena Russo, in front of whose cottage the *Etrusco* was stranded, for opening her house and furnishing gallons of coffee to those who had spent the long stormy night outdoors. It was in the enclosed front porch of her home also that Admiral Lebbeus Curtis later set up his shore-side office from which he directed the salvage operations.

The *Etrusco,* the largest vessel ever wrecked in the vicinity of Scituate, soon became one of the most publicized New England marine disasters of the century. During all of April and May she lay undisturbed on the Scituate beach, a mecca for sight-seers. Then, on June 26th it was announced that the owners, the L'Italica DiNavigazione, would start plans to cut the freighter to pieces. On August 16th, however, it was reported that representatives of a Norwegian shipping firm were planning to refloat the craft.

The Norwegian firm, known as the Global Shipping Company of Panama, was one of ten bidders for the vessel, and was given the right to go ahead when Clark-Wichert, insurance adjustors, accepted their bid above the other nine.

Immediately Transport Technique, of New York, American representatives of the Norwegian firm, through their spokesman, Captain J. Arenfeldt Johannesen, announced that they would arrive the following week to begin work. Admiral Lebbeus Curtis, who had salvaged more vessels than any other man in history, with a record of taking 1,040 wrecks off unfriendly shores, would be in charge of operations.

The salvage experts arrived in Scituate and set up their center of operations in the cottage across from the wreck. On August 30th Admiral Curtis stated that he would refloat the *Etrusco*, probably within sixty days.

Bulldozers began working at low tide around the wreck, clearing away the giant rocks and boulders which might later prevent a perfect launching. Within a week visitors could see the artificial jetty of rocks and boulders which the bulldozer had pushed above the surrounding sea bottom.

Four huge ship's anchors were successfully placed on the bottom about a thousand feet out to sea, with strong steel cables connected through blocks to winches on the ship. Compressors aboard the *Etrusco* were to turn the winches in the hope of pulling the ship seaward. The vessel's own anchors and chains were also ready to be used to help in this maneuver.

The hard strenuous work involved in getting a giant

freighter off the shore began in earnest on Sunday, September 23, 1956, when the compressed air tanks were tested as soon as there was sufficient water around the ship. At high tide, which was ten feet five inches high and occurred at 1:50 P.M., the crew tested the cables.

Pulling actually started on Monday, September 24th, at which time the bow of the *Etrusco* moved 1½ degrees seaward or from 177° to 175½° on the ship's compass. After co-operating unofficially for several days, on October 1, I signed on with the crew as a working historian of the project, anxious to do anything to make the trip to Boston.

The trying struggle with the sea was kept up in all kinds of weather, in many cases four times every twenty-four hours, at the two high and the two low tides each day.

To prevent excessive leaking the workers poured cement into the bilges, and with the aid of air pressure Admiral Curtis was usually able to control the amount of water coming in at any given time. Gradually, by pulling on the cables, the *Etrusco* was pivoted from a position parallel to the shore until her bow faced almost directly out to sea.

When large rocks were discovered under the ship, they were dynamited and their fragments removed. When dynamiting proved impractical, men crawled under the huge hull to place chains around the rocks, which were gradually yanked from under the ship by bulldozers.

The area around the bow and amidships underwater was dynamited. Then the bulldozers dug a channel running parallel to the *Etrusco* between her and the shore, several feet deeper than her keel.

Hydraulic and pneumatic dredging by powerful jet hoses also proved highly profitable in removing the concrete-like clay ridges on which the after part and amidships of the *Etrusco* lay.

One afternoon, when it was nearly dark, I was sitting on the porch of the Russo cottage when Captain Vlaho Bruer came sliding down the line in the boatswain's chair. Excitedly he ran up the few steps and shouted to me.

"Get out there with your canoe, I am afraid they are sinking." Slipping off my coat and rolling up my trousers, I ran down to the shore, slid the canoe into the water, and started taking strenuous strokes with my tandem paddle. I didn't know what was going on.

Two minutes later I was approaching a strange sight. Captain Bruer's son Gino and Captain Arenfeldt Johannesen were in the cumbersome punt which the Italian crew had built to go back and forth between ship and shore. Both Gino and Captain Johannesen were bailing desperately, and they were sitting astride several hundred feet of steel cable which was more than the small craft could carry. The captain's outboard motor was trying strenuously to move the sinking punt toward his objective at the end of the long breakwater before the punt submerged completely. There was an old sea running, with waves making up five and six feet high, and it was extremely doubtful whether they would make it.

They saw me coming in the canoe, and when I drew up alongside Gino slid into my other seat and grabbed a paddle.

"Am I glad to see you," shouted Captain Johannesen, "for I really don't know how they got me into this mess. I told them there was too much cable, and they said that there would be just a little more. After that they sent down at least two tons!"

We signaled for the crew to come out to the end of the breakwater and maneuvered my canoe between them and the punt to sustain enough weight of the cable to prevent the punt from sinking. This was done as the giant waves surged in and almost broke over the canoe. I steered my craft with its heavy load right up to the breakwater. A crewman up to his hips in the water, got a good hold on the cable end, and with the aid of a companion hauled it up on the riprap which forms the breakwater. Then the others took hold, and soon we were dodging the long, slithering heavy steel line which was being pulled across the canoe. Finally the last of the several hundred feet of cable left the punt, coiled its way across our boat, and plunged into the surf, to be hauled up on the breakwater by eight soaking members of the *Etrusco* crew.

Another day, I took two of the men assigned to dynamiting, Jerry Thomas and Lou Bailey, out in my canoe with a load of explosives. The purpose was to blow up the boulders that lay between the *Etrusco* and the sea. There is something about dynamite and dynamite caps which I do not enjoy, especially in a metal canoe leaving from and landing on a rocky shore in waves three and four feet high. Nevertheless, there we were, a hundred yards off the bow of the freighter.

Every so often Jerry would go over the side to set the dynamite. Whenever there was an explosion, stripers and codfish would rise to the surface, temporarily stunned, and if we were fast enough, we could catch them for dinner before they came to.

Finally the day arrived when the work out beyond the bow was finished and we were up in the forepeak of the

Etrusco. Dynamiter Bailey had fired several charges after Jerry had set them under the boulders to be destroyed, but then came the dreaded moment when the charge did not go off. This meant Jerry had to go under water to find out *why* there was no explosion.

But Jerry didn't waver a moment, and he was soon swimming over to the spot below the bow where the charge was planted. He dove under water, and disappeared for twenty seconds. Then he rose to the surface with the dynamite sticks, which were hauled up into the forepeak and examined. It had been a frayed wire which caused the misfire. This was repaired, the charge was set off, and the hazardous work of dynamiting was ended without injury to anyone.

There was ever-increasing curiosity about this salvage operation and even mothers with babes in arms would turn up in the middle of the night to watch. The comments of some of those spectators were priceless, and many thought that their own ideas were far superior to those of the admiral in charge. Others wrote and telephoned to give him the benefit of their plans for removing the freighter from her rocky berth. These included filling the ship's double bottom with hundreds of thousands of Ping-pong balls, raising the stern and pushing the hull off the beach with hydraulic jacks, and constructing a dry dock completely around the vessel. Possibly the most unusual suggestion was to lift the stern with the aid of helicopters and dirigibles.

After midnight the watchers became relatively few. Mrs. Dorothy Perkins, a newspaperwoman on the *Quincy Patriot Ledger,* describes her experiences as an early-morning spectator as follows:

"Assigned to cover the salvage operation whenever I felt it necessary and inspired by the claim of at least one salvager that a huge boulder under the engine room was the one obstruction holding the ship, I was on the job at 2, 3, and even 4 A.M. for several mornings during the final low-tide phases of the work.

"Of the 500 or more hours I spent at the site, these were perhaps the most weird. Perched on any reasonably dry rock at the water's edge, I was the sole spectator. In the water, the 'bazooka gang' were working furiously with their high-pressure water and air hose contraption to remove rocks and hardpan from beneath the ship.

"Not normally a scare-cat, my imagination began to work overtime. I continually 'felt' that someone was behind me. Hasty glances over my shoulder revealed only the steep, bulldozer-made hill, pushed up during the channel excavation and Scituate Light, always a quiet sentinel at the top in the sometimes scanty moonlight.

"Relief came when the generator ceased its racket for a coffee break. Then I could talk to the work team as I knelt in the wet and oozing sand to distribute cups, coffee, cream and sugar from a bucket which substituted as a picnic basket. I was a grateful, although nervous hostess— and far from beautiful in my damp jeans, stormcoat and ear-lapped cap."

What to me was the fever pitch of the entire operation took place on the night of October 18, when a strong northeasterly gale hit the coast. Among those participating on shore while Admiral Curtis was aboard that night were Captain Vlaho Bruer, and John Donlin of Marshfield, who is employed at the Bethlehem shipyard in Quincy. Captain Bruer indeed proved himself a man of the sea during those three excitingly vital hours when it seemed that the ocean was doing everything possible to smash apart the freighter. He and Donlin worked as a landside team to do whatever they could to get the vessel off.

Gigantic seas smashed again and again into the *Etrusco*. Even above the roar of the wind Captain Bruer's mighty voice could be heard giving orders. For a time the hopes of everyone were high. The tide reached its height, however, then started to go down, and there was the derelict, battered and bruised from the gale, but still in her regular position. It was a disappointing failure for all concerned.

The *Etrusco* began inching her way seaward on November 15, 1956, but it was not until three days later that any real progress was made. That Sunday morning brought an unexpected northeasterly gale with high seas. First the *Etrusco* started to pivot, with her fantail sliding seaward several feet as her bow moved toward shore. Suddenly this motion stopped, and watchers on the shore noticed a new unusual quiver shake the vessel, which had been pitching and rolling in violent fashion. Then without warning one of the cables reaching from the ship to the beach snapped. The *Etrusco* suddenly started out to sea in a southeasterly direction. She gained at least fifty feet, and was in the channel which the bulldozers had dug for her alongside of the clay ridges where she had clung.

Admiral Curtis then decided to flood her forward holds to prevent her from becoming unmanageable, and she settled to the bottom in her new location. Gradually the sand filled in around her shoreward or starboard side, and the tide went down. The following day was spent in attempting to pull her seaward, but as all efforts failed, hydraulic dredging under her hull with powerful hose lines was again employed and continued on Tuesday.

On Wednesday, November 21st, at high tide, the tag line grew taut. I was ashore at the wall, it being my pleasant task to let the line out as the *Etrusco* slowly moved seaward. The freighter gained fifteen feet. Then it was believed that the high tide of the next day, Thanksgiving Day, would see the *Etrusco* afloat. The morning dawned clear and seasonably cold. The compressors started and soon the cable lines tightened. The vessel moved seaward almost at once, slowly at first, and then by feet instead of inches.

By prearrangement, when the *Etrusco* reached a substantial distance offshore, it was my assignment to leap into my canoe, the only means of communication between land and the freighter, and to report to Admiral Curtis to find out whether or not a call for the tugs from Boston should be made.

I paddled out, went aboard and reported for orders to the admiral who was standing on the flying bridge.

"Send the tugs," he shouted, and I was off. Running down to the ladder, I jumped into the canoe with such force the seat crashed through and the crowds ashore thought I had gone overboard.

Landing on the beach, I rushed up to the telephone office in the residence of Mrs. Russo and asked Dorothy Perkins, holding the fort as it were, to telephone for the Boston tugs.

Then I dashed back down on the beach grabbing my movie camera as I did so, and went out in the canoe to the *Etrusco*. She was almost afloat by now, one hundred feet out to sea from her earlier position.

Tying the canoe to the ladder, I scrambled up into the

freighter just in time to miss the pump of number-three hold which then dumped several tons of water into the canoe, snapping the line. Meanwhile the *Etrusco* was slowly describing a giant circle with her stern, and was actually afloat by 2:40 that afternoon.

For those technically minded, Captain J. A. Johannesen prepared at my request the following statement of his plans for that vital day of Thanksgiving, 1956. It may add some information for those who are ever faced with a similar situation.

April 3, 1957

Dear Mr. Snow:

According to promise I am forwarding an exact copy of work planned on the *Etrusco* salvage job for Thanksgiving Day, November 22, 1956. This was written at 4:00 o'clock the same morning. High tide for that day was 1352 in the afternoon:

"Work all forenoon. Secure jet pump, machinery, booms, etc. on deck.

Pump out all holds, except No. 1 and fore peak.

Fill more water in No. 1 through deck line.

Overhaul all tackles full length.

Pull in port anchor as much as possible to straighten out chain and then slack off.

Pull ship 3 degrees or 2 rivets bearing on beacon with starboard breakwater wire about 10 feet.

Put wire aft for bulldozers to steady stern.

Telephone for tug for 3:00 o'clock P.M. readiness."

Sincerely yours,
with best regards,
J. A. Johannesen

There were some nervous moments aboard ship while we waited for the Boston boats to appear, but finally the tug *Orion* began pulling the *Etrusco* toward Boston at 4:20 P.M. with a second tug standing by. Two other tugs joined her off Boston Light, and after several narrow escapes the *Etrusco* was warped into Pier One, of the Bethlehem Steel Corporation at East Boston, at 9:25 P.M.

The saga of the *Etrusco* was over. She had made the port for which she sailed nine months before, but in doing so had spent eight of those months stranded on the Scituate shore. Repaired in Baltimore, she now sails the high seas again. To the admiration of all who witnessed the feat, Admiral Curtis had won his million-dollar gamble with the vengeful sea.

Incidentally, at a colorful ceremony a few days after the *Etrusco* reached Boston, the vessel was rechristened *Scituate* by Miss Ann Tilden, daughter of Representative Nathaniel Tilden of Scituate, thus honoring the town where the freighter had spent the greater part of 1956 high on the beach near Scituate Light.

THE MINERVA AT MARSHFIELD

Captain James Scott, an English mariner, married Mary Richardson on July 14, 1760. As Captain Scott was at sea a good part of the time, Mary went to live in Marshfield with her brother Jeffrey Richardson II and his wife.

On March 4, 1787, Mary's brother was suddenly awakened about three o'clock in the morning.

"Brother Scott has arrived and called to me," he told his wife.

"Go back to sleep," she admonished, "for it is only a dream." Jeffrey Richardson, however, was strangely troubled.

"It was more than a dream," he replied, but agreed to go back to sleep.

A short time later he heard his brother-in-law call to him again. The terror in his voice prompted Jeffrey to get up. Looking at the clock he found it was about half-past three. Dressing hurriedly, he went to the door and, when he opened it, was met by a swirling blizzard.

From the appearance of the high drifts around the house it evidently had been snowing for some time, and he noted from the northeasterly direction of the wind that it would be a fearsome night for sailors on the ocean, especially if they were off a lee beach.

Jeffrey went back to his bedroom, strangely disturbed and again awakened his wife.

"I am sorry, my dear, but I simply cannot get James from my mind. There is a great snowstorm outside from the northeast, and I am afraid that he is in serious trouble."

"What do you think you should do?" asked his wife. "It will not do any good to awaken Mary and get her to worry about it, will it?"

"No, perhaps not, but I am going to go down on the shore as soon as it gets lighter."

Jeffrey lay down without taking off his clothes and fell into a fitful sleep. About six o'clock that March morning such a mighty blast shook the building that he awakened at once and leaped to his feet. Glancing outside, he noticed that it was still snowing but by now the first gray streaks of dawn were lighting up the sky in spite of the severe storm.

Jeffrey ate a quick breakfast, said good-by to his wife, put on every storm-breaking garment he possessed, and left the house. It was a long walk to the Marshfield shore, but by seven o'clock he reached his destination.

A terrifying sight met his gaze. In every direction great masses of wreckage were strewn along the beach. Dead bodies were coming ashore, mixed in with seaweed and fragments of timbers. Others were already exploring the beach, and Jeffrey approached one of them.

"Not a soul escaped alive," the man told Jeffrey, "and I don't think anyone was on the beach when she hit!"

"What was her name?"

"I don't know, but the lighter stuff floated ashore down near Cut River, and the quarterboard might be there. It is a terrible thing, isn't it? Not a single survivor!"

Jeffrey walked down the shore, stumbling through the wreckage and the snowdrifts, until he came upon an area where the timbers and cargo were piled up three feet high. Several men were busily salvaging equipment from the surf and stowing it above the reach of the tide. Walking up to one of them, Jeffrey asked about the name of the vessel. One of the workers pointed to the south.

"We did come across fragments of the quarterboard," he explained, "but you'll have to piece them together."

Jeffrey went in search of these bits of wreckage, and soon he came across what had once been the last two letters of a word, ending in VA. Continuing his hunt further, he found a section bearing the letters I, N, E and R. The evidence was incontrovertible. Captain Scott's craft was named the *Minerva*.

Sick at heart, Jeffrey walked up and down the shore for the remainder of the morning. His wife and Mary Scott arrived at the scene shortly before noon, and he could postpone no longer telling them the terrible news, that Captain Scott had been drowned almost within the sight of his own home.

All three were spared the shock of watching the men working on the shore rescue the body of Mary's husband from the waves at low tide, for they had left the beach by then. Just before dark the remains of the master of the *Minerva* were carried to the church, and the family was notified shortly afterward.

Captain Scott's body was so marked by the surf that it was difficult to recognize him, but a large watch which he always carried with him confirmed the identification.

This watch was kept by his widow for the remainder of her life. She moved to Essex Street in Boston shortly after the tragedy and is believed to have died there about 1820.

Her children grew and prospered, and one of them inherited the watch. It is now in the possession of Roscoe E. Scott, at present a resident of Cleveland, Ohio, from whom I was able to receive many particulars about this strange story of mental telepathy and death.

Jeffrey Richardson was never able to prove that his brother-in-law spoke to him at the time of his wreck, although he was always very impatient in later years with those who questioned his story.

THE LEGEND OF THE NORTON

THERE ARE MANY WHO REMEMBER the great Portland Gale of 1898, but few who were out in another terrible hurricane which devastated our Atlantic coastline ten years before are still alive. A moderate snowstorm had been predicted for November 25, 1888, but in its place, from Portland to Cape Cod, came a fierce combination of sleet, freezing rain, hail, tremendously high tides and mighty surf.

As I have mentioned in a previous book, there were many spectacular marine rescues that day led by Captain Joshua James * of the Hull Life Saving Station, including those saved from the *Cox and Green,* the *Gertrude Abbott,* the *Bertha F. Walker,* and the *H. C. Higginson,* but the story of the fishing schooner, *Edward H. Norton,* has never been told before in the fullness it deserves.

Shortly after midnight on November 26, 1888, a patrol-

---

* *Mysteries and Adventures Along the Atlantic Coast,* page 204.

man noticed wreckage, including dories, smashed lumber and other debris, coming ashore near First Cliff in Scituate. Going down to the rocky beach, the surfman found a dead body floating in, and pulled it high above the reach of the sea. Rushing back to the Hull Life Saving Station, he notified the other life savers, and they soon arrived on the shore opposite what apparently was the wreck of a fishing craft, the 73-foot *Edward H. Norton,* hailing from Wellfleet, Massachusetts.

Out on the vessel, only one man was still alive. He was Martin Allen, a fifty-year-old seaman of 2 Wiggin Street, Boston, who had a wife and three children awaiting his arrival there. A seafaring man for 31 years, he had been with his fifteen fellow sailors aboard the fishing craft when the gale hit Massachusetts Bay that Sunday morning. By dusk, as he later explained, everyone knew they were in for a terrible night. The first mighty sea smashed into the *Norton* at six o'clock that evening, and when it was followed by another and still another, each one as bad as its predecessor, Allen felt that the heavily loaded vessel would not survive. After less than ten minutes a terrific billow completely engulfed the *Norton,* and over she went, capsizing with horrifying suddenness in the blackness of that November night.

Allen was washed down into the forecastle, where he clung desperately to a line, being smashed back and forth against the bulkheads, until half-past seven the following morning. Each wave that crashed into the vessel pushed it closer to the shore.

Finally the *Norton* hit the rocky beach at the base of First Cliff, just across from the lighthouse, and Allen thought that he would never survive. By this time the water was neck-deep in the capsized forecastle, and the imprisoned sailor was almost unconscious. But he still held on to the line, although his wrists had become numb in the freezing water.

He had no way of telling the time, but the tide could be ascertained more or less by the force of the waves. When it began to go out around three o'clock that morning, Allen noticed that as the billows receded, the lee side of the vessel would begin to rise, for she was in the trough of the sea.

This movement was accentuated as the ebb increased. Although terrible seas were still running, Allen thought that he might have a chance to squirm out under the rail should the roll of the *Norton* become greater.

Still, under the hull of the overturned fisherman, he knew that his chance of survival was indeed very small. He would have to free himself of the lines, waiting until the exact moment when the hull rolled enough for him to slide under, and move fast enough so that he would not be caught by the next wave, which would inevitably pin him down, break his back, and leave him to drown.

Finally came the wave for which Allen waited. As the water engulfed him to his chin, the seaman cut his lines. He then clung to the bulkhead, waiting for the backlash of the wave to strike the *Norton*. As the receding wave took the hulk temporarily in tow, the schooner lifted its shoreward rail just high enough for him to squeeze underneath before it settled back on the bottom again.

With a prayer on his lips Allen squirmed out, swam and kicked his way to the surface of the water, and struck out for shore. The following wave caught him when halfway to his goal, swept him in toward shore and then out again, and smashed him against the hull. This time, however, he was on the outside of the wreck.

Pushing off from the schooner, the seaman swam and floated toward shore, getting almost up on the beach when another wave caught him and hurried him in toward land. As it started out again he grabbed in desperation at a rock, and his hand caught on a cleft in the surface of the boulder. There he clung as the wave left him, but he knew that his respite was for only a moment.

Summoning all his waning energy, he tried to gain his feet, but found that he didn't have the strength to stand erect. With the sound of another oncoming breaker behind him, he rolled over and over, each time moving upon higher ground. The billow caught him, raced beyond, and then subsided, but he was near the limit of the wave's surge, and the water left him high and dry.

With victory over the ocean in his grasp, Allen, by sheer nerve, then moved himself another ten feet and reached the seawall. There he became delirious. Shortly before seven forty that morning he was seen by residents of Scituate. Rescuers carried him to the residence of John Conroy, where he was given aid by the owner and his wife.

At midnight the first body from the disaster washed ashore and was picked up on Stage House Beach by the life savers. It was later identified as one of the Frenchmen in the crew who had signed on at Prince Edward's Island. At nine o'clock the following morning Captain Frank Curran's remains washed ashore. The master of the *Norton* was identified by his bushy red hair and beard.

It is believed that Captain Curran had put his fourteen-year-old son Mike in the cabin, and when he later rushed below to save the boy, the two were drowned. The father's body, which evidently had floated free from the cabin, was found hopelessly pinned by timbers, ropes and nets. He still carried a paper on which was a short prayer to the Holy Virgin.

After Allen escaped from the vessel, the life savers decided to break into the hull with axes. When this was done, the body of the captain's son was found and pulled out through the opening.

On learning the details of Allen's thirteen-hour nightmare in the forecastle of the *Norton,* old-time fishermen of Scituate said that without question his struggles were "the most horrible experience they ever knew a man to go through."

Regarding the storm, veteran life-saving captain, Fred Stanley, in charge of the Scituate Fourth Cliff Life Saving Station, made the following statement:

"It is the worst storm I ever saw, much worse than the one during which Minot's Light went down. That storm came during a high course of tides, while this one came on a low course, which makes a big difference on the force of the waves. Why look at that meadow!

"On a high course of tides the meadows would be overflowed anyway, but this storm on a low course even has made a difference of four or five feet in the harbor."

The story has been erroneously told that Allen was actually rescued through the same hole cut into the hull of the vessel, by which the body of the captain's son was extracted, but I have the signed testimony of the only survivor, Martin Allen, made after his complete recovery, describing his miraculous escape. Excerpts from this statement follow:

"I was washed down into the forecastle, where I clung to a rope all night . . . About seven thirty this morning I crawled out as a sea ran back, and got to shore . . . They picked me up on the wall."

A FAMOUS GALLEON OF 1616

ONE OF THE EARLIEST marine disasters of which we have recorded knowledge is that of an unknown galleon, probably French, which sank in a great storm in the year 1616. Her bones were scattered along the shores of Marshfield from Ocean Bluff to Brant Rock. Only one man was saved, and his name is believed to be Peter Wallis. Captured shortly after the wreck by Indians, Wallis was taken to what is now Middleboro, then called Nummastaquyt, where he remained as a captive for three years.

Then on May 19, 1619, Captain Thomas Dermer set sail from Monhegan Island in "an open Pinnace" and "passed along the coast" to arrive in Plymouth. Finding all the Indians dead from a plague, Dermer "travelled alongst a daies journey Westward" until he reached Middleboro, where "I redeemed a Frenchman."

Peter Wallis, the redeemed Frenchman, was allowed to settle in what is now Pembroke, where his orchard and his well can be seen to this day!

Back at Marshfield the great galleon slowly went to pieces at the bottom of the sea, and it was not until around 1880 that a chance dive brought the old wreck to light. At that time a friend of the late Adelaide Hildreth Burgess of Brant Rock owned an expensive shotgun. He lost it one day while out on Brant Rock hunting ducks and summoned a diver down from Boston. The diver never found the shotgun but among other things which he brought up were two blunderbusses and a cannon from the ancient galleon. Later, cannon balls and grape shot were found in the area, the last grape shot being discovered by Parker Phillips of Brant Rock several years ago.

Mrs. Burgess told me shortly before her death that a fragment of the old wreck was reputedly buried close to the Brant Rock ledge itself. The keel of the galleon was discovered after a storm in 1953 had scrubbed out the sand from the area, and diving operations have been going on from time to time ever since.

Diver John Light has made the most important find. At dead-low tide on December 6, 1953, he went overboard at the scene of the wreck where a buoy connected to a grapnel at the bottom had been placed. His statement follows:

"On December 6 I descended to the bottom in 35 feet of water off Brant Rock. I found the grapnel, which was stuck between two rocks. I freed it, came back about ten or fifteen feet and found myself on something which was hard, smooth and even. It seemed like metal or rock. I went down eight inches with my right foot. I was facing west, in the general direction of the boat.

"I got my other foot off the object, but the visibility was only six inches. The water was extremely roiled because of the recent storm. I knelt down beside the object,

turned around, and faced back. Then I examined it and
found that I could push my arms way inside under the
object.

"I found that the object was of metal, man-made, about
two inches thick all the way. It was about nine feet from
one end to the other, and six feet across. It came out
of the mud at a slant. The object appeared to be a great
slab of iron. It wasn't jagged but smooth and could very
well have been the iron caboose of a galleon.

"After I examined it I ran into the fluke of what was a
very large anchor. It was probably about ten feet long,
possibly fifteen feet. It was about fourteen inches out of
the sand, and apparently came out of the sand at a slight
angle, indicating that the other fluke, from the size of the
one showing, was directly below, about eight feet distant.
The fluke was from four to five inches thick."

That December day, I interviewed fisherman Charles
Newton of Island Street, Brant Rock, who told of two
more anchors, one in Brant Rock Cove and the other in
the area right off Blue Stone at Ocean Bluffs. One of
the anchors was very large and heavy and had a wooden
crosspiece. Newton and his brother Bob had hooked on
to the anchor and dragged it in about one hundred yards
when the line parted and they had to leave it there. The
other anchor, relatively close to a location off the Mullen
residence, had the fluke and part of the arm showing out
of the mud in about twenty-five feet of water at half tide.

When John Light found the metal fragment, he set the
grapple underneath and buoyed the location. All the following winter of 1953-1954 Jim Mullen, who was flying in
a plane over the region, noticed the buoy bobbing up and
down in the water. Unfortunately a March northeasterly
swept in across Brant Rock and the buoy was snapped

off. Repeated attempts to relocate the metal fragment have failed, possibly because sand has now covered the location to a depth of from four to seven feet, according to the estimates of lobstermen who fish in the vicinity. Several thousand dollars' worth of pieces of eight may still be at the bottom there.

In 1953 an old shield, fragments of a conquistador's helmet, a small anchor and more than a score of pieces of eight were recovered and brought to the surface. On Wednesday, August 24, 1955, it was reported that C. Thomas Burgess, Jr., fourteen-year-old skin diver whose summer house was fairly close to the area, went down to the bottom and recovered a heavy, water-soaked fragment of the ancient vessel. Later I presented that same fragment of the 1616 shipwreck to Warren Strong to be exhibited at the Pilgrim Museum at Plymouth, where it is today.

There are those who have a good knowledge of historical ships who believe that this metal part of the galleon was the old iron caboose of the ship. Probably, if there is treasure still aboard, the bulk of it is in this vicinity.

In order to recover additional relics or curios from this wreck much more work is necessary, and success depends on the storms which sweep in across New England during the winter months. Possibly some reader of this chapter may become wealthy by finding the bulk of the treasure aboard this seventeenth-century French galleon, but I must offer my usual admonition—the chances of this happening are extremely remote.

20

INCIDENT AT CLARKE'S ISLAND, OR AMERICA'S FIRST REAL THANKSGIVING

FEW OF US REALIZE the unusual chain of events which led the Pilgrims to decide eventually on Plymouth Harbor as their location for a settlement.

Briefly, the *Mayflower* had arrived at Cape-End Harbor, or Provincetown Harbor, as we call it today, on November 11, 1620. The women had later gone ashore to do a great washing, while the men made plans to explore the area.

Many historians claim that the Pilgrims had intended to settle in Virginia originally, and while they were at Provincetown Harbor they changed their minds and decided on Massachusetts. I have always believed that they had the idea of a New England settlement from the beginning, and merely talked about Virginia from start to finish while planning otherwise. The reason is that while

163

New England offered them a wilderness, it is true, there would be neither an established Anglican church (as there was in Virginia) nor an established government (which then existed in Virginia).

In any case, the men brought a longboat, called a shallop, ashore at Provincetown and began to repair it for a voyage of exploration. Meanwhile a party of sixteen set off hiking and exploring. They eventually returned with corn stored by the Indians which they had found on the way.

At last the shallop was ready, and thirty-three men went aboard under the command of Captain Jones of the *Mayflower*, who had been named chief of the expedition because of his "kindnes & forwardnes."

The shallop reached Corn Hill, where they had earlier found corn on their first exploratory hike. With the aid of cutlasses and swords they broke through the snow and frozen ground to gather a great abundance of corn, which they brought back on the shallop to Provincetown.

The corn so pleased those on board the *Mayflower* that there were many who now suggested settling at Corn Hill. Mate Robert Coffin, however, told the others of Thievish Harbor, which was much more suited than Corn Hill for a settlement.

The morning of December 6, 1620, found eighteen men aboard the shallop, their intention being to sail up the coast until they entered Thievish Harbor and then to go ashore. Among the eighteen there were ten Pilgrims who had volunteered to make the trip with the crew, including Robert Coffin, William Bradford, Myles Standish, Stephen Hopkins and John Carver, who became the first governor of Plymouth colony. Stephen Hopkins had taken along his servant, Edward Dotey.

It was a bitter-cold day, typical of December, with a hard wind hitting across Massachusetts Bay. The spray whipped up out of the water and froze into ice on their clothes, which turned to "coates of iron." Several of the men became sick "unto death" from seasickness, while others fainted from the cold. They went ashore that night somewhere along Wellfleet Bay and discovered where Indians had been cutting up a huge black fish. While camping that night on shore, they were attacked by Indians, but fortunately they were able to fight off the intruders.

The next morning another high wind hit the coast, but the Pilgrims pushed off from shore. Soon it was snowing hard, and by midafternoon an easterly gale was lashing the area. At the mercy of wind, waves and the snow, which obliterated all coastline, the Pilgrims were in desperate straits. Suddenly a great billow smashed into the shallop. The strain on the rudder proved to be too much, and it snapped off so that the men were unable to keep the craft before the wind. Two oars brought into service made it possible to hold a course of sorts.

They were approaching land, and since darkness was settling over the ocean at the time, it was agreed that they should put up more sail and take a chance on getting into harbor before night fell. Suddenly another towering wave smashed into the shallop. The mast broke into three pieces and toppled overboard with the sail in what was described as a "very grown sea." Working like mad, the men cut away the fragments of mast and sail and thus avoided capsizing.

Then probably off the Gurnet, their situation was not one to be envied. Relentlessly the wind, waves and incoming tide swept them along in the pitch blackness of the night. Then, without warning, the roar of mighty breakers was heard. All aboard could see through the darkness the whiteness of surf rolling shoreward on a rocky beach. Mate Robert Coffin, who had been reassuring the others with remarks that he believed he knew where he was, now abandoned all hope.

Just as the shallop was about to be swamped by a gigantic comber, one of the sailors took momentary charge of the situation. Grasping his steering oar firmly, he shouted at his fellow seamen: "If you are men, about with the shallop, or we are all cast away!"

The others steadied their oars. Rowing with superhuman efforts for about five minutes, they rounded a point of land I like to believe was Saquish, and finally found themselves in the lee of a large promontory. In the blackness of the night they decided that they had better stay aboard the shallop rather than go ashore and face an attack by more Indians, which the Pilgrims called a "huggery."

Soon the wind shifted to northwest, and it became much colder. John Clarke, acting first officer, announced that he was going ashore anyway, and he and several others were soon landed in the rough surf. They lighted a fire, and one by one the others joined them and warmed themselves. When morning came they found that they were actually on an island (later named Clarke's Island for John Clarke) in Plymouth Harbor. Exploring, the Pilgrims discovered a huge rock, which still stands on the island, and climbed to the top.

As it was then Saturday, they agreed to rest there, dry out their gear and conduct a service of thanksgiving on the rock, in which they would give the Lord "thanks for His mercies, in their manifould deliverances."

I like to think of this thanksgiving service at the giant rock as the first real Pilgrim Thanksgiving. I often visit the giant boulder which still remains unchanged and unmoved, not at all like its sad companion, the famous Plymouth Rock itself, which has traveled many hundreds of feet and has lost many hundreds of pounds from its original weight.

Early on Monday morning, December 17, three hundred and thirty-seven years ago, the Pilgrims sailed back toward Provincetown in their repaired shallop and reported to the rest of the company that Plymouth Harbor was their choice as the location for a settlement. And so it was that a party went ashore from the *Mayflower* on December 18, 1620, landing not very close to the large boulder on the shore we have come to call Plymouth Rock.

THE LEGEND OF
WHITE HORSE ROCK

MY FIRST CLOSE GLIMPSE of White Horse Rock at Manomet in Plymouth, Massachusetts, was back in the year 1936 when I was on a leg of my trip from Gurnet Light to Cape Cod in my annual Christmas role as Flying Santa, dropping packages to the Coast Guardsmen at lighthouses and coast guard stations.

We flew in low over the large boulder and noticed that there was something painted on the side of the rock which faced the shore, but we could not make out what it was from the plane.

Later I visited the area by driving down to Manomet and turning off on the road which led to White Horse Beach. Nearing the location, I stopped just before reaching the ancient White Horse Hotel, and was attracted by the handsome wooden statue of a white horse in plain view through the large plate-glass window on the second floor of the hotel.

The story of this animal for which the rock, beach and hotel are named is found in a venerable legend of the area, which I determined to track down.

But first I visited the giant boulder known as White Horse Rock, almost half a mile offshore. I discovered that boys traditionally paint an American flag on it every year, the day before the Fourth of July, and that is what we had seen from the air. After the painting is finished the young artists dive into the sea and swim the long distance ashore.

Having visited the rock, I spent the next two hours interviewing everyone in sight about the history behind the name. I found that even the lobster fishermen knew very little of the background of the story, and it was two weeks before the entire tale was revealed.

The main source of the White Horse legend, I found, lies in a fourteen-verse poem written about three quarters of a century ago by Timothy Otis Paine, pastor of the New Jerusalem Church at Elmwood, Massachusetts. He was known as one of the great scholars of his day, having assisted in the translation of the Rosetta Stone. He also wrote a volume entitled *Book of Solomon's Temple.*

The White Horse poem concerns two young lovers, and the story actually begins the year before that part covered by Paine.

In 1778, twenty-year-old Roland Doane shipped aboard the armed privateer *General Arnold* at Boston under Captain James Magee. Doane was one of the crew when she sailed away on December 24th in company with the privateer *Revenge.* Reaching Gurnet Light, Captain Magee found that a severe storm was developing, and anchored his vessel less than a mile from the lighthouse.

Unfortunately, by morning, the gale strengthened, and the weather became very cold. The captain ordered sixteen of the vessel's twenty guns lowered belowdecks. The topmasts were struck and the sails snugly furled. Long scopes were given to the anchor cables, but the waves rose higher and higher. Finally the *General Arnold* began to drag anchor.

Suddenly, with a quiver which jarred the vessel from stem to stern, she grounded on the sands of White Flats. The masts were cut away, but giant sea after giant sea smashed the wreck. The seams began to open up, and soon the cabin was three-feet-deep in water. Forced to flee topside as best they could, the sailors braced themselves for the freezing weather. Meanwhile the entire Plymouth Bay had frozen solidly with pack ice.

As the afternoon wore on men began to die from the cold. The seas mounted in fury, until each wave brought a sheet of icy spray which froze solidly to the clothing of the crew huddled on the deck. At nightfall many of them gave up hope entirely, and about fifty perished before dawn.

When morning came those who were still alive made a shelter out of the bodies of their dead comrades, and crawled inside for warmth. With daylight, the survivors noticed that men from Plymouth were constructing a causeway out over the ice floes. Two hours before noon the rescuers were within hailing distance of the wreck, and soon the sleds and boards were pushed alongside the brigantine. One by one the frozen sufferers were taken ashore. Roland Doane was one of the twenty-four of the crew of 170 who survived, but he had suffered severely from frostbite, and a Mr. Paine, a resident of what is now Manomet, agreed to nurse him back to health.

Roland's benefactor had a daughter named Helen. She was quick to take over the duties of nurse, but the patient's improvement was slow. First the weeks and then the months went by with Roland still convalescent.

It was August, 1779, when Roland was finally strong enough to leave the Paine homestead. By this time he and Helen had fallen in love, but her father refused to allow a marriage to take place. Taking matters into their own hands, the two lovers escaped from the house one afternoon and were married in a nearby town. Then they returned before the father was aware of their absence. Roland left the following day, after planning to anchor his schooner offshore on the night of August 24, 1779, to pick up his bride.

Paine completes the story in his poem, "The Legend of Helen of White Horse":

I

Where beach plums waxen green and swell,
'Til rich October ripes them well,
And Cape Cod Bay her sand dunes reach,
Heaps high along her White Horse Beach,
Far back in thick old Plymouth fogs,
Love bloomed as flowers bloom in bogs.

II

But not as plums were good to eat,
In Plum Glen where lovers meet—
Where Helen keeps with Roland tryst,
And lips have touched in love and kissed,
For it was August, and the growth
Of fruit and love lacked much in both.

III

The fruit lacked purple mellowness,
And love lacked cleric hands to bless;
For Helen's father would not bear
To give his child to Roland's care,
And Helen could not bear to part
With all there was in her one heart.

IV

And so she told her father so;
And every evening she would go
And meet with Roland on this road
Tradition tells Myles Standish trode;
This sunken road that used to run
Between two homes, once meant for one.

V

Where the Alabama cot now stands,
The dune is one sharp ridge of sands
Protected by the tops and roots
Of beach-peas, grasses and the shoots
Of barberry bushes, and woodbine,
And thickets all along the line.

VI

Below your feet, a deep down dell
Is red with roses, sparrows dwell
Secure on ground and bough;
Eludes the searcher's half day quest.
Poor Helen's home was near this spot,
Between the neighboring pond and cot.

VII

And this is Beach Plum Glen! The sea
Sounds in the dell incessantly;
One bound this rugged height out o'er
The sparrows feed along the shore,
And toward the Gurnet's double light
The White Horse Beach is full in sight.

VIII

The twenty-fourth of August dawns,
T'was young in ages long agone,
And Helen's love was young and strong,
And life is love and love is long;
Young Roland must to sea again
And meets bride Helen in the glen.

IX

His jaunty cap and sailor dress,
His bearing high, his manliness,
Were much to lose and sail from shore,
Poor Helen thinks, "Forevermore."
And she must bear her father's pride,
Her own loved Roland far awide.

X

She warns her father yet again,
That he will grieve, but warns in vain.
The night shuts down and it is dark,
The midnight comes; the parents hark,
They listened once before to-night
And thought they heard before; were right.

XI

Her bed had not been occupied,
The father could not find the bride;
The white horse was not in the stall,
The saddle, bridle gone and all.
He hurries, shouting, to the beach;
The white horse swims her out of reach.

XII

"Come back, my daughter!" loud he cries,
"I will no more oppose!"—but dies
The cry upon the sounding sea;
The white horse moves out steadily;
And Helen nevermore returns,
Nor beacon light for Roland burns.

XIII

Where Beehive Cottage stands beside
The road that leads down to the tide,
But out to sea, a massive block
Hath long been called "The White Horse Rock."

XIV

But love will let no lovers die;
And oft in all these years gone by,
Upon her steed, and late at e'en,
Bride Helen on this rock is seen
Looking for Roland through the mist
Until he joins her keeping tryst.

22

THE SAGA OF THE
SPARROW-HAWK

ONE OF THE MOST FASCINATING subjects about New England is the large number of ships which have been wrecked or stranded on or off her shores. I actually have listed and charted in a general fashion the remains of about 1700 such disasters.

Among these is a small craft, commonly known as the *Sparrow-Hawk*, that made headlines of a sort in the famed William Bradford's journal at the time the tiny Plymouth colony was struggling through the year 1626. The vessel, roughly estimated to be 40 feet long, had sailed from England for Virginia in the fall, with about thirty persons on board.

Toward the end of a weary passage, during which their provisions were exhausted, the commander, Captain Johnston, fell ill "and lame of the scurvy," according to William Bradford, so that by this time all he could do was to "lie in the cabin door and give direction." Losing track of his position, he headed his ship for the nearest land and thus passed over the shoals of Cape Cod to enter "a small blind harbor" called Manomoyick, now known as Pleasant Bay.

Although it was then high water, the *Sparrow-Hawk* touched on a bar of sand. According to Bradford, the vessel "had no hurt, the sea being smooth; so they laid out at anchor." By evening, unfortunately, the wind sprang up and the craft was pushed across the bar into the harbor and ran ashore on the flats.

The crew and passengers were wet, thirsty and hungry, and their firewood was exhausted. At low tide they began to unload their goods on the dry shore.

A short time later Indians approached them by canoe, and the little group on the Cape Cod beach wondered what might be in store for them. They were greatly relieved when the Indians spoke to them in English. The red men asked the sailors if they were friends of the Pilgrims, and plans were soon made for a trip to Plymouth. The leaders of the expedition, Mr. Fells and Mr. Sibsie, sent two men with the Indians to deliver a letter to Governor Bradford at Plymouth, asking for help in the form of food and other supplies.

Arriving in Plymouth, the messengers were received courteously by the governor himself, who on ascertaining the serious plight of those on the *Sparrow-Hawk* soon packed a boat with provisions and started across Massachusetts Bay.

By this time several of the seamen had taken up with the Indians and had "run away." Governor Bradford soon had them back, however, and within a few days Captain Johnston was ready to sail again.

Instead of starting immediately for Virginia, as he had originally planned, the captain of the *Sparrow-Hawk* for some reason first went into several other harbors on Cape Cod, "and loaded his boat with corn which he traded."

Finally, when he was about to sail to his final destination in Virginia, Captain Johnston ran into such a violent gale that the *Sparrow-Hawk* was pushed ashore on a lee beach right inside the entrance to what is now Pleasant Bay and was wrecked beyond recovery.

Thus it was that the tiny Pilgrim community was forced to receive the survivors at Plymouth and provide food and shelter for them, among whom were several Irish servants. With the coming of winter, the group helped clear additional land for planting corn, and did very well at the harvest the following summer and autumn.

A scandal, however, rocked the settlements, when it was discovered that one of the two leaders of the *Sparrow-Hawk* expedition was paying too much attention to a young girl who was one of his servants. The two fled first to Cape Ann and later to Boston Harbor, attempting to escape the wrath of the Pilgrim community but to no avail for no one would take them in. Finally the Pilgrims arranged for the leader's transportation with the girl back to England.

Governor Bradford, after telling the above story, goes on to say that "ther were allso some that caried them selves very orderly all ye time they stayed," and finishes by explaining that "a cu ple of barks caried them away at ye later end of somer. And sundrie of them have acknowledged their thankfullnes since from Virginia."

Captain Johnston's stay in Massachusetts was barely one year in duration and when he sailed away he left the wreck of his vessel still at Cape Cod.

The years went by. Inevitably, the craft was covered over by the sand, which the tides filled in around her nearly to the decks. The wind completed the burial of the *Sparrow-Hawk* and within a few years of her stranding she was completely submerged.

People began to call the location of the wreck Old Ship Harbor. During the great December 4, 1786, gale which did so much damage up and down the Massachusetts coast, the surf washed the sands away from the wreck, uncovering it for the first time in over a century and a half, and Cape Codders of the period were able to obtain a view of this ancient relic of Pilgrim days. Nothing was done, however, at this time toward removing the old vessel to a permanent resting place.

The War of 1812 and the Mexican War came and passed into the annals of history, and then the Civil War began to tear our nation asunder. On May 6, 1863, two men were hiking Nauset Beach on Cape Cod. They were Solomon Linnell and Alfred Rogers, both of Orleans, and during their walk they had reached a point a little to the northeast of Strong Island. Suddenly they noticed blackened timbers sticking up a few inches above the surrounding marsh mud.

Excited by their discovery, an historically minded Cape Codder named Leander Crosby went to the wreck. There he began a scientific survey of the remains of the ancient craft. Day after day Crosby dug carefully in and around the vessel. His research uncovered "a quantity of beef and mutton bones; several soles of shoes, probably made for sandals; a smoking pipe of the kind used by smokers of opium; and a metallic box."

Dr. Benjamin F. Seabury and John Doan, Jr., afterward discovered the rudder of the wreck lying "a few feet distant," and had it removed to "the hall of the Pilgrim Society, at Plymouth."

The excitement of the discovery spread far and wide. Soon many people were making the long four-mile trip out from Orleans Village to view the remains of the craft.

The following August saw the wreck again covered by sand, but when in the fall the seas laid her bare once more, patriotic citizens assisted in moving the remains of the *Sparrow-Hawk* above the reach of the sea. The fragments of the wreck were then sent to Boston by Charles W. Livermore for assembly by the shipping firm of Dolliver & Sleeper.

On August 17, 1865, the firm reported to Mr. Livermore that the original length of the vessel on deck was probably about forty feet. It was also stated that her keel was of English elm and the floor timbers were of oak. It was ascertained that the planks had been scorched on the inside, "and then suddenly saturated with water for the purpose of bending them into shape as a substitute for the modern method of steaming."

A few days later Mr. Livermore received a letter from D. J. Lawlor, who stated that "she must have been an easy-sea boat, and well adapted to the carrying of passengers."

The bones of the venerable patriarch among ships was then placed on Boston Common, opposite to Temple Place, where it was on exhibition for several months. Then the *Sparrow-Hawk* was transported to Providence, at the suggestion of Mr. Livermore, where it was again exhibited to the public.

Around the year 1880, according to Secretary Warren P. Strong of the Pilgrim Society, the remains of the vessel arrived in Plymouth, and were stored in the Chilton Street side of the lower hall. When the hall was enlarged the *Sparrow-Hawk* was set up in the basement room there, which came to be known as the Sparrow-Hawk Room.

In the year 1952 the Pilgrim Society asked H. H. Holly to examine the vessel and reassemble it correctly. Mr. Holly completed his task in admirable fashion, and the ancient ship is now as nearly in its original shape as possible.

There is no direct evidence to confirm that this craft was actually called the *Sparrow-Hawk*, for her name was never officially revealed within a century after she was wrecked. As the remains were found on land settled by the Sparrow family less than fifty years afterward, it is possible that they christened this interesting relic, but barring information to the contrary, it is as good a name as any.

23

THE LEGEND OF SCARGO LAKE

IN THE YEAR 1946 I spent several weeks hiking around the shores of Cape Cod, covering in all about 235 miles by a means which today is considered almost obsolete— walking.

One day, in the distance, I sighted the tower of Scargo Hill, located high above Scargo Lake. I had often seen this structure from the air during my Flying Santa runs over the lighthouses at Christmas, and here was a chance to visit it.

After passing through East Dennis, I turned left on the Scargo Hill Road and was soon climbing. The hill and the tower were up at my right. Finally I reached a smaller path which came out at Scargo Hill tower itself.

I was carrying with me a poem about the famed Scargo Lake, which had been published in the *Cape Cod Magazine* in 1922. I pulled it from my knapsack and began reading it aloud. The author of the poem was unidentified, and as the *Cape Cod Magazine* had gone out of busi-

181

ness, I had no way of finding who was the writer of this version of the legend.

The poem tells of the Indian Princess Scargo, who was the beloved daughter of Sagauw, chieftain of all the Nobscusset Indians. The girl's mother had died at the birth of Scargo, and this tragedy had so impressed itself on the mind of Sagauw that he became obsessed by a resolve to protect his daughter from the thought of death in any form.

Several years later the chief from a neighboring tribe brought some live fish as a present to the girl, and the tiny, squirming creatures made the child very happy when they were placed in a small pool near her home.

The following spring, unfortunately, was without rain, and the sun dried up the pond, killing almost all the fish. Although she was not told what happened the little princess instinctively realized that many of her pets were dead, and it made her very sad. Despondently, she was able to save several of the live fish from the pond and placed them tenderly in a bowl at her home.

She was overcome by the thought of the dead fish, however, and in her sadness, Princess Scargo began to waste away. Finally, Chief Sagauw told his ailing daughter that he would build a mighty fish pond, one that would be as wide as an arrow's flight and would never dry up. At this promise from her father, the Indian princess began immediately to show signs of improvement, and eventually recovered her health completely.

Then came the day when Princess Scargo was to officiate at the shooting of the arrow. A brave chosen for the event stepped forward. Drawing his bow taut, he shot the arrow, which described a sweeping parabola in the heavens and then dropped down to earth.

The princess obtained two giant sea-clam shells and placed them carefully, one at the point where the Indian had stood and the other at the spot where the arrow hit the ground. A corresponding distance was agreed upon for the length of the lake and soon the entire tribe started work on the project of scooping out the earth.

Day after day, week after week, men, women and children dug out the dirt and transported it away, working in the hot sun and the chilling rain without letting a day go by, for it was all for their little princess.

Finally, late in the fall, the great lake was finished. Alongside it, reaching high into the heavens, was an enormous mound of sand, made from the excavations.

Thus were formed Scargo Lake and Scargo Hill. When the late autumn rains began to strike Cape Cod, the lake was soon filled to the brim and the princess tenderly transferred the fish from her bowl to their new home. As the years went by Scargo Hill was eventually covered with trees and foliage. The fish prospered and had many descendants, which to this day can be found in the Indian-made lake.

The tower on the top of Scargo Hill, rising twenty-eight feet above the mound, was built about the year 1912 by James Allen Ellis for Charles and Frank Tobey to replace an earlier wooden tower they had constructed.

After finishing the poem, I visited a small granite marker some distance from the lake which probably identifies the final resting place of the great Chief Sagauw and his daughter, for whom the tribe made their gift back in the days when no white men roamed the wilds of Cape Cod.

Eleven years later, I still had been unable to find the name of the author of the pleasant poem concerning "The

Legend of Scargo Lake." Then, on January 26, 1957, I opened a letter from Ella Hall Eldridge, of Middleboro, Massachusetts, which informed me that her uncle, Captain Marcus Hall, of Dennis, Cape Cod, had written the verses which I quote in their entirety below:

The Legend of Scargo Lake

Scargo was an Indian maiden,
 Lived here centuries gone by.
Brown her cheeks as leaves in winter
 As the wild dove was her eye.

And her father's name was Sagauw,
 Chief of all the fair Cape Land.
Oak and pines then waved their branches
 Where is now but barren sand.

And the chieftain loved this daughter,
 She, the apple of his eye,
Childish wish or maiden fancy,
 Nothing he could her deny.

Youngest she of all his children,
 Daughter of his favorite squaw,
Who had joined the untold numbers
 When the light this dear child saw.

And to please this mighty chieftain,
 When the tribes were not at war,
Presents wrapped in bark and deerskin,
 Came from near and from afar.

Presents dear to Indian children,
 Gaudy box or carven dish,
Or a little bow and arrows,
 Or some cunning little fish.

And one day there came a runner
From a far and distant tribe,
And he bore a mighty pumpkin,
Carved by cunning Indian scribe.

On the outside was the totem,
On the inside all scooped out.
In some water there was swimming
Little perch and dainty trout.

And the child expressed her pleasure
In ways that Indian children know,
Hopped on one foot, then on tother
Scratched her left shin with her toe.

Then she scooped a little fish pond,
Carried water in a dish.
When 'twas finished to her liking
In it placed the treasured fish.

But there came the long dry Springtime
All the brooks and streams ran dry.
Scargo's fish with gills wide opened
Turned them on their sides to die.

Then the little maid grew frantic,
Wrung her brown hands in despair.
With white clay she daubed her forehead,
Then cut off her tangled hair.

Then she howled and woke the echoes
In each ear she stuck a leaf.
And another in each nostril
But they brought her no relief.

Sagauw called his squaws together,
Grave old dames with toothless smiles.
"Get your fire-sticks, get your punk-wood,
Make a smoke to show for miles."

Then they twirled and twirled the firesticks,
    Turned to left and turned to right,
Till the wood grew hot and smoking,
    And at last it was alight.

Then with breath and bough they fanned it,
    Coaxed it with pine knot and cone,
Then threw green pine needles on it,
    Sagauw said, "Old gals, well done."

And the smoke curled high in air,
    Stretching far off toward the West,
And the warriors knew its meaning,
    Hastened at their chief's behest.

Sagauw clad in robes of deer skin,
    Skunk-skin cap upon his head,
From the hill watched with his daughter,
    She had cried her small eyes red.

"Father, can you see the braves?"
    Wailed the sad-eyed little maid.
"You can bet the boys are coming,
    Skookum-Sinash," Sagauw said.

O'er the bay in bark canoe,
    From the West by forest track
Came the warriors, came the squaws
    With papooses at their back.

With the young men came the maidens,
    Decked with flowers to make them fine.
And the children with the dogs
    Stretched in a far reaching line.

Then the warriors greeted Sagauw,
    Each man waiting scratched his head.
And with gracious Indian manner
    "Oot Sutch Semma," Sagauw said.

Then they had a mighty pow-wow,
  Sagauw told them of his plan
That the squaws should dig a fish pond,
  And they grunted, every man.

Then the young men went for clam shells,
  Scargo marked her fish pond site.
And its breadth by Sagauw's promise
  Was to be an arrow's flight.

Scargo chose the strongest warrior
  When the wind was at the north,
Twanged the bow-string on wrist leather
  As he sent the arrow forth.

Scargo watched the arrow falling,
  Placed a shell at either side,
Cheated some on East and West side
  Got it longer than 'twas wide.

Now came trailing o'er the meadows
  With such loads they scarce could wag,
Brown and naked little fellows
  Weighted down with cat-tail flag.

And the squaws began their weaving
  Baskets by the lunched score,
Piles on piles of giant clam shells
  Packed the young men from the shore.

Scargo restless and impatient
  With a clam shell in her hand,
Dug and scooped and scarcely rested
  Till a trench was round her land.

Then the squaws began their digging,
  With their shells they scooped the sand,
Piled it in their woven baskets,
  Dumped it out upon the land.

"Hurry, hurry," screamed the child,
    Up and down the serried rank,
Patient creatures how they waddled
    With their baskets up the bank.

Days and weeks the sands kept piling,
    Days and weeks in broiling sun,
'Till the Autumn was approaching
    And the mighty deed was done.

And the rains came with the Autumn
    Poured as though 'twould never stop.
Scargo sitting on the sand heap
    Watched her pond fill to the top.

She, by the most patient tending
    Of the perch had saved a few,
Night and day she carried water
    All that long dry Summer through.

Now she placed them in the pond,
    Watched them as they swam away,
There they are, or their descendants
    Swimming to this very day.

On the bank of her loved water,
    Guarded by the States bequest,
There beside the "Scargo Villa"
    The chieftain and his daughter rest.

And on quiet summer evenings,
    At the far side of the lake,
Calling gently, "Scargo, Scargo,"
    Then the echoes will awake.

Where the shadows lie the deepest
    Loving couples often pause.
They are listening to the echoes,
    'Tis the grumbling of the squaws.

A MIRACLE OF THE SEA

THE SEAPORT OF PROVINCETOWN, Massachusetts, located far out on the end of Cape Cod, has witnessed tens of thousands of arrivals and departures of almost every type of vessel. Equally at home in the spacious Cape-End Harbor, as it was once known, were mighty men-of-war of the British fleet and the present giant warships of our American Navy.

In the year 1803 a trim eighty-ton fishing schooner named *Polly* sailed from Provincetown Harbor. Bound for the Bay Chaleur,* she carried ten sailors. Among his crew Captain Peter Rider had brought along with him his nephew, the ten-year-old cabin boy Ned Rider.

The voyage was Ned's first trip, and long before the tall church at Provincetown faded into the distance he began to wish that he had stayed at home where he could put his two feet on a surface which did not roll. As the

---

* Inlet between Quebec and New Brunswick.

Polly continued her journey up the coast, passing Thacher's Island and the Isles of Shoals, Ned became more and more seasick. Then, as the days went by, he slowly recovered and began to lose the feeling of giddiness. By the time the *Polly* had reached Mount Desert Rock, young Ned had fully regained his enthusiasm for the sea.

Finally they left Sable Island behind, and a few days later reached Bay Chaleur. The fishing for the next few days proved highly successful, surpassing the most optimistic hopes. Soon the last basketful of salt had been wet and the long fishing lines were back on the reels. Now that the *Polly* had a full hold, the hatches were battened down and Captain Peter Rider set his course for the journey back to Provincetown Harbor.

Two days later, early on a Sunday morning, the *Polly* was becalmed off Saint Paul's Island which is located some ten miles to the northeast of Cape Breton Island. As she drifted along with the current, Ned came up on deck and stood by the rail. He watched intently as the sea gulls wheeled back and forth over the stern, and as he was listening to their almost plaintive cries, he heard a new sound in the distance. It resembled for all the world the lusty yell of a young child, but where could it be calling from out on the broad Atlantic?

There was a large rock offshore from the main body of land known as Saint Paul's Island, and Ned wondered if the voice could be coming from there.

Rushing below, he aroused Captain Rider and told the veteran mariner what he had heard. In order to humor his nephew, the captain agreed to come up on deck and listen to the noise the boy had heard. As soon as he reached the rail, Rider paused and heard only the cry of the sea gulls as they twisted and turned above the stern.

He was then ready to dismiss the incident from his mind.

"That's what you heard, lad. It was a sea gull, make no mistake. Some of those gulls have a different sound from the others and that is what alarmed you."

But just as he was preparing to go below again, there was another pitiful cry. This time it apparently did come from the distant rock, and even the captain was impressed with the humanlike quality in the sound. He decided that he would get two of his men to row over to the rock and investigate.

Ned jumped in with the two sailors who had been chosen, and soon the men were rowing toward the pinnacle. Still becalmed, the *Polly* scarcely moved on the glasslike surface of the sea as the men neared the rock.

Five minutes later the rowboat reached its destination, and Ned clambered out. There was nothing in sight at first, and so he climbed around to the other side of the boulder. Then it was that he heard the cry again, this time from a distance of just a few feet. In less than a minute he had reached the spot from where the sound came. It was a small niche in the giant ledge, which was rapidly being engulfed by the oncoming tide. There, just about to start crying again, was a frightened little girl. The tide was already coming in and her body was wet to the waist. It was not long before she would have been swept away by the rising sea.

Climbing down from the pinnacle into the niche, Ned took the little girl's hand. Carefully he pulled and led her up over the sharp points to the top of the rock. Then, hand in hand, they descended the other side. The men in the boat gasped in astonishment when they saw what Ned had found.

The girl and her rescuer got into the boat, and the

sailors rowed away from the rock. Nearing the *Polly*, they attracted the attention of the crew. Captain Rider stood by the rail ready to receive the dripping child, who was now crying steadily from fear, excitement and relief.

"Well, now," exclaimed the captain, "how did such a little girl as you get off on that rocky ledge so far from shore?"

The child's only answer was another series of sobs. As the cook brought some warm chocolate, the captain's bunk was prepared for her so that she could take a nap. Her wet clothes were removed, and one of Ned's heavy shirts served as a nightdress. Ten minutes later she was asleep.

The men, however, gathered at once to discuss this remarkable occurrence. How could such a thing happen? Who would wish to maroon a tiny child on a niche in a lonely rock out in the Atlantic where the tide would soon drown her?

"I'd give anything to catch the man who did this thing," said Ben Smith with a vengeance, "for either he or I would go overboard!"

"In any case," said Captain Rider calmly, as if he had already appraised the situation, "it is true that we don't know how the girl got on the rock, or where she came from, but I for one am not going to try too hard to find out. While we're not exactly fixed for a nursery aboard, at least we are far more human than the critters who left that child out on the rock to die."

And so it was decided that the *Polly* would have a little girl aboard for the remainder of the trip. Shortly after midnight Monday morning a breeze sprang up, and by dawn the *Polly* was speeding along at seven knots, bound for Provincetown Harbor with as strange a cargo as ever a Cape Cod fisherman had taken from the sea.

By the time that the *Polly* was abeam of Thacher's Island, the crew had voted to name the child Ruth, in memory of Ruth Adams whose father, one of the crew, still mourned her death three years before. When they sailed into Provincetown Harbor and rowed ashore, great was the astonishment on the faces of the women of Cape-End Harbor to see a tiny girl step out of one of the boats.

It had been agreed that Ruth would be quartered at the residence of Ned's grandmother. Captain Rider, whose wife had died, lived with his mother and his nephew Ned, whose own parents were dead, and the child proved a welcome addition to the family. As time passed, she looked upon Ned, who was seven years older, as her brother.

In the summers Ned went fishing, and in the fall, winter and spring he attended school. Finally, his education ended and he took command of the *Polly* from his aging uncle, who told his friends that he was happy to retire from the sea and "stay ashore for a spell."

As his interest in Ruth grew, Ned became anxious to discover what he could concerning who the girl was and where she came from. The next time he was in the vicinity of Saint Paul's Island he went ashore but found to his disappointment that no one lived on the island at all. However, he did discover evidences of several shipwrecks, and later learned that the island had been the scene of many terrible disasters in its early history. Nevertheless, from all he could gather, the child must have been left on the rock during calm weather, as there had been no evidence of a shipwreck nearby at the time she was found.

Back at Provincetown, when Ned returned from the trip which had taken him ashore at Saint Paul's, he went at once to his home. With a cry of delight Ruth met him at the door and threw her arms around him. Then, shyly blushing, she drew back and looked at him with a new awareness as she realized that she no longer considered him like a brother. Now about sixteen years old, for of course her exact age was never known, she appeared to be a grown woman.

Thus it was that Ruth and Ned recognized their true affection for one another. Ned explained at once what he had been doing at Saint Paul's Island, and ended by telling her of his failure to find out anything about her.

Ruth, having known for years that she had been found at sea on a fishing trip, sensed what Ned was leading up to when he talked about her background. After a long discussion he suddenly proposed that they get married and she accepted him at once. The entire town turned out for the wedding, and Captain Ned Rider built the pair a new house, one of the finest on Cape Cod. They lived happily ever after, unconcerned by the fact that her mystery was never solved.

A decade ago I visited Saint Paul's Island and learned that some years after Ruth had been found, a lighthouse had actually been erected on the rock. Located across a natural channel of water from the main part of the island, it is now connected by a cable car to Saint Paul's itself.

Several generations of the descendants of Ruth and Ned now populate Cape Cod, and many others have migrated off-Cape. For those grandchildren and great-grandchildren, this will always be an intriguing story.

GRAND MANAN

Up and down the New England coast, on islands, in deep water where ships have gone down, along sandy shores which have borne the tramp of pirate feet, and in forests located not far from the sound of the mighty ocean, probably $200,000,000 worth of treasure is located. Of course, most of this wealth will never be found, but because of improvement in treasure-seeking devices, it is safe to say that where even ten years ago only about $5,000,000 of that $200,000,000 was salvageable, today at least three times that amount can be detected and taken from its hiding place.

I have a series of master charts which indicate the location of untold wealth. The next step, however, to bring it back into circulation, is the hardest one of all, and the legend I give in this chapter is a typical example.

Grand Manan Island, which is situated about six miles out to sea from West Quoddy Head Light, is the site of one of the queerest stories ever told concerning a hunt for buried treasure. On September 2, 1821, a strange vision appeared to a woman named Hunt who was living on nearby Campobello Island. She was known as the Widow Hunt, for when the story begins her husband, a sea captain, had been lost at sea three years. It is said that she always believed he would return to her and help her make her living.

The Widow Hunt had been thinking of her husband one evening just before she went to bed, and it was that very night that she had her dream. A boy of dark skin appeared to her, stripped to the waist, but headless. Despite his affliction, the boy addressed her in a calm, cool voice.

"Go to Grand Manan Island," he instructed. "There you will find Money Cove. Be sure you have a compass with you. You will see a rich treasure of gold, if you go into the woods alone and do not look behind you. Once in the woods, you will find a beaten path making up over the hills on a southeast course. Do not make a mistake, but be sure you go southeast.

"Keep account of your distance traveled. When you have gone 500 feet I will be there awaiting you. Then I will take you to the scene of the buried treasure. When we reach the location a mighty wind will spring up, and that will be our greatest danger. Whatever happens, do not falter."

When Mrs. Hunt arose the following morning, she thought that she had just had a terrible nightmare. She did mention her dream at the breakfast table but her listeners were not unduly concerned.

She could not forget the vision, however, and when she retired that evening thoughts of the headless lad were still in her mind. Once more her sleep was troubled by the

same experience in an exact duplication of the night before. When she arose the following morning and told her
story, she explained that the colored lad showed such a
"singular, friendly eagerness that she could not treat the
incident with skeptical indifference."

Word went around Campobello Island of the Widow
Hunt's strange dream visitor, and many of her friends
came to her and gave her advice. Some cautioned against
doing anything, impressing her with the possibility that it
was only the vividness of her first night's dream that made
it return the second night. Her relatives implored her to
do nothing foolish, as it might bring ridicule upon the
entire family. A small group of visitors, nevertheless, suggested that the only way to settle such an affair was to
follow the advice of the Negro lad.

Then came the third night. The lad appeared again,
but this time he seemed aware of what was going on in
the mind of the Widow Hunt.

"Seeing that apparently you have some doubt concerning my words," he began, "why not give me a chance to
demonstrate my ability? I am in communication with
your husband, and can prove it. Put me to the test!"

"I will," she replied. She thought quickly of something
that had happened between her and her late husband
which no one else knew about. She recalled that just before he sailed away, he had lost a hatchet. She had looked
for that tool many times since but had never been able to
find it.

"Tell me," she said, "where my husband lost the
hatchet, and if it be so, I will believe in you and do what
you say."

The headless lad told her at once that if she went out
behind the large woodpile in the rear of the barn she

would find the missing hatchet placed exactly on the "eastern end of a six-inch-wide board which is ten feet long."

The next morning the Widow Hunt and her entire family went out behind the barn and found the hatchet exactly where the headless lad had told her it would be. The entire island of Campobello was aroused when word became known of this last visitation and the remarkable discovery that resulted.

The little group which had been anxious for her to follow through and visit Grand Manan now insisted that she should go, especially as she had promised the vision that she would. Four strong men volunteered to accompany her as far as the forest, and a boat was provided for her use. Most of the Campobello Islanders implored her to forget the entire affair, and soon it was necessary for the five to make their plans in private.

On the sixth day of September the Widow Hunt and her four protectors sailed away from Campobello, arriving the same afternoon at Whale Cove on Grand Manan, where they went at once to the residence of a man they all knew who ran a boardinghouse. He agreed to put them up and let them use his building as a headquarters. The host was somewhat amazed that Mrs. Hunt would be allowed to visit Money Cove at night, and he also felt that she was conducting herself as though a supernatural force was compelling her to act contrary to her own inclinations.

At ten o'clock that night the five people left the house, making their way down to the beach. There they climbed into a skiff and started rowing toward their objective. Passing Eel Brook, they proceeded out around Northern Head as quietly as they could, for it was a calm night and ordinary sounds could be heard for some distance.

Even the noise of a distant waterfall could be detected tumbling down over the great cliffs of the island toward the sea. The huge, dark mass of Grand Manan stood out in the starlight, ominous and threatening. The Widow Hunt soon fell under the spell of the occasion, oppressive and sinister as it was.

"Could we have spoken," she said later, "it would not have been so terrible, but I had been told not to talk. Had it not been for shame and the fact that I had already caused my four friends a great amount of trouble, I would have turned back, even though the entire island were made of gold!"

They landed the skiff on the northeastern end of the great seawall, and the Widow Hunt was now shaking visibly as they stood there. Then she began walking slowly along the top of the seawall. Trembling, she dared not look behind her, and those who were watching expected her to faint at any moment.

Then, gathering courage, she braced her shoulders, walked ahead with a cheerful step and disappeared into the woods. No sooner had she entered the forest than a strong, bright light struck the area around her. As far as she could see, it was shining all through the forest. Then away in the distance, the headless lad could be seen. His body was facing toward her, and he was sitting on what apparently was a treasure chest.

Suddenly, the calmness of the weather vanished. She felt first the faint zephyrlike breath of wind brush against her face, and then it became stronger. Harder and harder the gale blew, until soon it was a tempest! The pine trees all around her began to roar and a hurricane lashed the forest in great strength.

Then the light grew dimmer, and she lost sight of the

vision. New, indescribable fears now assailed her. She
later explained that she never understood what gave her
the strength to continue walking. "I knew not what I was
doing," she explained.

Now the woods began to echo and re-echo with the
noise of a great battle between two forces. She could hear
the clashing of swords and cutlasses and the shouts of the
victors mingled with the groans of the dying.

"I could not think, nor could I see the boy on the
treasure chest or even the great bright light while this
terrible fighting was going on!" Then came the most
frightful part of the entire affair.

"The unearthly yells and foul oaths seemed more as if
from demons than human beings, when all of a sudden
there burst in full sight, a hundred of the fiercest, most
murderous-looking brutes, cutting, trampling and tearing
at one another.

"But to make it worse they were now advancing toward
the spot where I stood, horror-struck and unable to walk.
There seemed nothing else left for me but that I would be
trampled to death or cut to pieces by the demons' swords.

"Then there came a weird flash of bluish lightning, and
it illuminated the entire scene of terror. Another and then
another flash followed it, and then there was the most
terrifying thunder I have ever heard. It shook the great
hills on the island with a sickening sensation, almost like
an earthquake.

"It was dreadful to experience, and I stood there
stunned and speechless. I struggled frantically to scream
for help, but my voice seemed to have left me utterly.
Every nerve was paralyzed, but I did scream once.

"It was then that I must have fainted, for I remember
no more until I awakened in the boat, where my four

friends were bathing my wrists and temples with water."

The four men had heard the scream and had to search for some time before they found her. They rowed Mrs. Hunt back to Whale Cove, where she was put to bed at once by the wife of the island resident. The next morning she awakened, and gradually her experience of the night before came to her.

Although questioned repeatedly as to what had taken place, her answer for a full year afterward was a refusal to discuss the matter. It was not until the fall of 1822 that she told the entire story just as it has been related here.

At that time the four men were then interviewed, and solemnly averred that they had experienced nothing of the wind that Mrs. Hunt mentioned, nor had they heard the sound of men fighting in the forest. It was then estimated that she must have been unconscious after her fainting for more than two hours before they found her in the forest.

In later years many expeditions visited Grand Manan and attempted to locate the treasure chest in the forest, but as far as can be told, all were unsuccessful, and for the remainder of her days, Mrs. Hunt never was troubled with further visitations of the headless lad.

Our story now jumps ahead to a period just before the American Civil War. By this time the Widow Hunt was an old lady, and quite willing to tell those who asked her of her experience on Grand Manan.

One day in 1859 there came a visitor named Samuel Alcott Ward, who said his home was in Lewiston, Maine. Deeply impressed by what she told him, Ward decided to delve into the matter further. A strong oarsman, he thought nothing of rowing the seven miles out to Grand

Manan from Campobello Island. When he landed his boat, he went to the house on the island where the Widow Hunt had stayed during her brief visit of 1821, and learned from the owner the approximate location of the dell where the weird events had taken place. Visiting the forest at Money Cove, he made a careful survey, and then he rowed away from the island.

Samuel Ward returned to Grand Manan on three more occasions in a two-week period, and then a year went by. About eleven months after his first visit he went back again, but this time it was by means of the Canadian schooner which served as island-to-shore packet for those who had business with Grand Manan.

Ward had brought along several heavy boxes, and engaged a rowboat in which to take them around to Money Cove. Soon he was rowing toward his objective with his cargo, and although those unloading the packet thought about it for a few days, other matters came up and they eventually forgot the incident.

Meanwhile Ward landed at Money Cove, unloaded his boxes on the shore, carried them up to his destination in the forest and returned to the beach. Then he rowed the boat back to the man from whom he had engaged it. That afternoon he rented a room at the boardinghouse where he had lived the preceding summer.

For the next two weeks he spent most of the time, even in the pouring rain, out in the dell at Money Cove. To those who visited him there he explained that he was conducting scientific experiments on echoes in a forest, but of course he didn't fool any of the natives with such an explanation. They knew what he was after—treasure.

Curious residents decided to investigate for themselves. One man in particular waited until Ward had obviously left the dell for supper at the boardinghouse and then the inquisitive islander went down to where the boxes were standing. He discovered that immediately behind them there was a new hole in the earth, thirty inches deep, and about four feet square, unquestionably dug by Ward.

No other part of the area had been disturbed, but one of the boxes had the cover pried off and inside lay a large slab of iron, about ten inches long, six inches wide and an inch thick. Lifting the slab, the islander found several like it beneath.

The following day the curious resident perched himself in a tree and watched Ward's activity from a distance of one hundred yards. The night before the spectator had tramped three miles to the home of a friend to borrow the prize possession on the island, a great telescope from the wreck of the ill-fated *Lord Ashburton,* lost at Ashburton Head.

All day long he spied on Ward, returning the following morning and the next day as well. Before Ward left Grand Manan that year the islander knew his entire secret.

Ward had brought out a magnetic device with which he conducted experiments in the forest dell designed to help him find a treasure chest. After burying the metal slabs, he attempted to locate them by the magnetic device. When he actually found the iron in this manner he then knew that he could locate the treasure chest by the same method. Obviously, he was satisfied with his experiments, for before he left the island that year he was starting on a systematic inspection of the entire dell. He had only covered one twelfth of the area when his vacation ended and he had to leave the island, storing his boxes in the cellar of the boardinghouse.

The following year he returned, but his vacation had been shortened, for the Civil War had broken out. He did little work, and after inspecting an area about three yards wide and two hundred feet long, he left again.

Ward did not come back until 1866. Having gone to war, he had been captured and incarcerated at Libby Prison. When he returned to Grand Manan he was so thin that at first no one recognized him. Nevertheless, he started out at once to make up for lost time, while the inquisitive resident was once more out at the scene, with the telescope, even though the intervening years had made it harder for him to climb the tree to his observation post.

Ward found nothing that summer, however, and he did not visit Grand Manan in 1867, for reasons best known to himself. But the following year he arrived at the island with still another box, this time a heavier one weighing over one hundred pounds! He transported it out to the scene of his operations, and was soon back at work. From his perch high in the tree, the persistent spy noticed that Ward was now able to move over the ground at a faster rate. Before his vacation ended, he had surveyed every part of the dell except a more-or-less inaccessible valley overgrown with young pines, quite a distance from the shore of Money Cove. This summer, he left the island on August 28, 1868, not to return until August 11 of the following year.

My theory, not shared by the natives of Grand Manan, is that by this time Ward sensed that some of the curious islanders who noticed his comings and his goings might be spying on his efforts. In any event, one afternoon early in September he visited the fishermen and asked if there might be a dory or boat he could buy. He found that one

fisherman would sell him a boat for $30. "I'll let you
know within two days," said Ward as he walked away.

Indeed, matters were approaching a climax. He returned to his dell, worked with his machine all that afternoon, and stopped his efforts at about the usual time.

Unknown to Ward or anyone else on the island, a gentleman on the mainland named Saxby had predicted a
short time before that a bad gale or hurricane was about
to hit the entire area.

The following morning when the tireless resident of
Grand Manan arrived at his tree, he noticed that Ward
was not working. The islander rambled down to the
boardinghouse, and as he had a speaking acquaintance
with Ward, asked for him.

The boardinghouse proprietor stated that Ward had
not come down for breakfast, and went up and knocked
at his door. There was no answer. The door was swung
open, and it was noticed that the bed had not been slept
in. Ward's suitcase was also missing.

Both men looked at each other. Now concerned, they
went across to the dell in the forest. After searching the
area, they were amazed to find a substantial hole dug far
inside the relatively inaccessible valley. The bottom of
the hole was about twelve inches by twenty inches in size,
and about thirty-six inches down. Whatever had rested
there had been iron, for the rust encrustations on the side
of the hole or pit were still plainly visible. There was no
sign of Ward anywhere.

As they were exploring in the valley a great wind began
to blow. Actually, it was the beginning of the famed
Saxby Gale. The two men hurried down to the fishermen
to ask about Ward and one of them told that his boat was
missing and he had found three ten-dollar bills fastened

to his bait house. Everyone then decided that early that morning, shortly after midnight, Ward had rowed away for the mainland, probably with the Widow Hunt's treasure aboard his boat!

That same day the Saxby Gale hit the entire coastal section of that area, causing untold damage and hardship. The residents on Grand Manan naturally wondered if Ward had survived the storm since neither he nor the boat reappeared.

Various estimates were made as to the value of the money in the chest, judging from the space it had occupied. If it happened to be all silver it was worth a paltry $36,000, but if it were gold, then Samuel Ward had probably found better than $300,000 worth.

But Ward, if he did reach the mainland before Saxby's Gale caught up with him, did not bother to communicate with the Grand Manan Islanders. He never returned, nor is there any record of his ever reaching his home at Lewiston, Maine.

What still attracts my attention is the fact that the winds of September, 1821, swept across Grand Manan at the time of the Widow Hunt's visit and exactly forty-eight years later, in September, 1869, a gale predicted by Saxby again swept Grand Manan at the time Ward left the island. Possibly Saxby should not get credit for the gale. There are many who may feel that the headless lad was the real culprit.

26

THE GASPÉE, OR WHAT REALLY
HAPPENED AT NAMQUIT POINT

THE COMPLETE STORY of how the British armed schooner *Gaspée* was taken by force and later burned can never be told in all its unusual details for the same reason that many of the facts concerning the Boston Tea Party, which occurred eighteen months later in Boston, will never be known.

Both the burning of the *Gaspée* by the people of Rhode Island and the throwing of tea from the three tea vessels * in Boston Harbor were done in times of extreme danger to the participants, for if anything had been revealed shortly afterward to the British, many of those taking part would have been hanged. Therefore it is no wonder that very few of the details were known for many years after each occurrence. In recounting the *Gaspée* affair, we are

* See my *Amazing Sea Stories*, p. 84.

aided by a broadside written within a year of the event, now a treasured possession of the Rhode Island Historical Society.

It is probable that the British themselves were at fault in the way they governed the American colonies. For well over a century Parliament had been making laws which regulated trade on the American side of the Atlantic, laws which told the traders what they were allowed to do and what they could not do.

But at the same time England made almost no effort to enforce those same laws, and gradually the colonists traded as they pleased, actually running their own lives and businesses with little thought of interference from across the sea.

The year 1763 saw a change in this British policy of laissez-faire, and the English began to enforce the laws more strictly.

It was one particular law which caused the most trouble, an act which stated that a tax or duty should be paid on many commodities which were important in the colonists' everyday life, including duties on molasses, sugar, tea and rum. When Lord Grenville, the British minister, discovered that the total revenues from colonial customs amounted to but two thousand pounds annually and that the yearly collection cost was no less than eight thousand pounds, he called for strict enforcement of trade and navigation laws.

The customs officers were now told that their days of relaxation were at an end, and from then on many of the goods which were almost openly being smuggled into Rhode Island and other parts of America were to be taxed. The colonial governors were also to be held to account if they did not aid the tax officers in every way they

could. Several armed vessels were sent across the ocean
to back them up. The *St. John,* the *Liberty,* the *Squirrel*
and the *Gaspée* were among those assigned to the Rhode
Island region.

At the time, the tiny area of Rhode Island owned more
vessels in proportion to her size than any other colony.
There were well over five hundred craft and two thousand
sailors to man them. In addition to the smaller vessels
which operated only in Narragansett Bay, the large,
stately ships which traded in foreign countries brought
back to Newport, Providence or Bristol great cargoes of
molasses, spices, sugar and silks. The owners of these
large craft particularly resented the fact that they had to
pay England a tax on goods they were bringing back to
Rhode Island, commodities obtained not in England but
other far-distant lands.

During 1764 the *St. John* came to Narragansett Bay and
proceeded to stop all craft and examine their cargoes,
fining the owners if it was found the duties had not been
paid. This constant interference with Rhode Island's com-
merce became such a nuisance that plans were made by
the inhabitants of Newport to destroy the *St. John.* In
the midst of this preparation, however, another armed
craft, the *Squirrel,* arrived to help out the *St. John,* and
the plot was temporarily abandoned. Two armed craft
at once were more than the people in Newport could hope
to eliminate.

There was action, however, that same year. The British
frigate *Maidstone* anchored in Newport Harbor, and a
group seized her longboats, carried them up to the common in front of the courthouse, and there set fire to them,
yelling and cheering as the flames consumed the hated
British craft.

Five years later the armed sloop *Liberty* made herself known by the severity of the examinations conducted by her master, Captain Reid. One day a Captain Packwood, whose brig's cargo was found to be fully paid in duties, had his clothes stolen from him and taken aboard the *Liberty*. Going to the sloop to retrieve his clothes, Packwood was lucky to escape with his life, for not only was he bodily abused aboard the sloop, but musket shots were fired at him on his return to his brig. Luckily, neither he nor anyone else was injured.

Captain Reid had not been aboard when the incident occurred. That evening he started for the Newport pier where his longboat was tied up, and he was threatened by a crowd of angry Newport men, who told him what had happened. He was informed that the *Liberty* was going to be destroyed, and he would be wise to get all his crew off his craft.

Standing on the pier, Captain Reid glanced from face to face and realized that the Americans were not bluffing. After a moment or two of indecision, he sent out word for his crew to abandon ship, and this order was carried out.

A short time later Newport sailors arrived at the *Liberty*, brought her into Long Wharf, took her boats off, cut her masts away and sent her to the bottom. As in the case of the *Maidstone*, the longboats were taken to the common and burned.

By 1772 there had been so many incidents involving British armed vessels and the people of Rhode Island had been so badly handled that the citizens needed very little encouragement to explode into armed aggression. The appearance in Narragansett Bay of the British schooner *Gaspée* in March, 1772, with Lieutenant William Duddingston in command provided a spark to set off the explosion.

Duddingston was arrogant, insolent and overbearing. It was a point of honor for him to make sure that he stopped all traffic in the bay. When tiny little market craft were held up and vegetables were tossed about in a search for rum or molasses, the farmers complained that much of their produce was being spoiled. If vessels did not stop at once on hail, a shot was sent across their bows. Duddingston apparently enjoyed the irritation of the farmers in small boats. Finally conditions became so bad that people were afraid to visit one another if it meant a sail across the bay.

Complaints soon came to the ears of Governor Wanton of Rhode Island that Duddingston was acting illegally in many cases, sending goods under question to Boston in spite of the Act of Parliament stating that all such cases should be tried in the same colony where the goods had been seized. He wrote a letter to Duddingston concerning the illegal acts and received a very insolent answer. Governor Wanton then wrote him another letter which was answered by Admiral Montagu in Boston who told him in even bolder words to stop interfering with Duddingston.

This was the state of affairs on June 9, when Captain Thomas Lindsey sailed his American schooner *Hannah* from Newport, bound for Providence. The *Hannah* had already been carefully examined by the British at Newport, but Captain Lindsey realized that Lieutenant Duddingston would probably attempt to catch his vessel and stop him as he sailed by the *Gaspée*.

All the *Hannah's* sails were spread as she approached Namquit Point. This is a long spit of sand about five miles south of Providence which makes its way out from the mainland just to the northeast of Occupessatuxet Cove. As Lindsey figured, he was challenged and then fired upon by the men on the *Gaspée*, but he paid no attention, continuing to sail toward Providence. The *Gaspée* started to follow the *Hannah*, and now in order to make sure of escape Captain Lindsey sailed in as close as he dared to Namquit Point.

Aroused and angry, Lieutenant Duddingston ordered his helmsman to cut across the spit in order to overtake the *Hannah*. Suddenly there was a grinding jar, and the *Gaspée* was caught on the sand bar. Duddingston had sailed too close to the point. To make matters worse for the British, the tide was on the way out, and soon the proud vessel began to career.

Captain Lindsey noted to his satisfaction that the *Gaspée* would probably remain aground until three o'clock the following morning at the next high tide. Arriving at Providence, he immediately set out for the home of his good friend John Brown to tell him how the *Gaspée* had run aground. Mr. Brown was fascinated by the thought that it was now in the power of the men of Rhode Island to destroy the hated craft, and the two men started formulating plans to accomplish this objective.

Two hours after sunset the roll of a drum was heard at the upper end of Main Street in Providence, and soon afterward it was announced by the drummer's companion that not only had the *Gaspée* run aground on Namquit Point, but that she would be there until three the following morning! "Those who wish," continued the speaker, "to go and destroy that troublesome vessel are invited to repair to the home of Mr. James Sabin this evening."

Again and again the drummer and his companion per-

formed their duty, so that before nine o'clock James
Sabin's Inn was crowded with eager men who had brought
their guns and pistols. Bullets were made in the molds
at the fireplace, and soon every person had arms and
ammunition.

Eight large longboats were rowed across to Fenner's
Wharf with all the rowlocks and oars muffled. By ten
o'clock the expedition set out with Captain Abraham
Whipple in command.

The tiny navy rowed out beyond Fox Point and then
reached Field Point. Next the longboats passed the
mouth of the Pawtuxet River and began to approach
Namquit Point itself, where the *Gaspée* lay keeled over
on her side. It was now almost two o'clock.

The longboat armada was within a hundred yards of
the schooner before the lookout aboard the *Gaspée* noticed them.

"Who comes there?" the marine sang out. No one
bothered to answer him, and the Americans now rowed
hard to make their goal.

Lieutenant Duddingston, hearing the challenge, hurried up on deck and cried out. "Who comes there?"

It was Captain Whipple who answered. "I want to
come aboard!"

"Stand off, for you can't come aboard," answered Duddingston, ordering his marines to start firing.

"I am the sheriff of Kent County. I am after the commander of this craft, and have him I will, dead or alive!"
answered Captain Whipple. "Men, spring to your oars."

As the British began shooting, Joseph Bucklin, a colonist
in one of the longboats, took careful aim at Lieutenant
Duddingston. Firing, Bucklin wounded the British leader
in the groin.

"I'm done for," shouted Duddingston, and for a few moments all sides began to fire at each other in the darkness. No one else was wounded, however, except a British sailor, who was hit in the head. The men of Providence soon reached the schooner, boarded her, and forced the surrender of the British seamen.

Lieutenant Duddingston was carried down into his cabin and given first aid by Dr. John Mawney, after which all the British were put into the boats and taken across to Stillhouse Wharf on the Warwick side of the bay.

Then it was that the men of Providence returned to the *Gaspée* and set her on fire in several places. Retiring to a safe distance, they watched the flames begin to lick up the deck and sides and into the rigging of the hated schooner.

Suddenly an explosion rocked the bay, for the powder magazine had blown up. Within an hour or so the blaze began to die out, as there was very little left of the *Gaspée*. Their task well done, the men in the eight longboats then rowed silently back to Providence. They separated just as silently and returned to their homes.

Of course, when the British leaders learned of this act of aggression, suitable rewards were offered for the apprehension of those responsible for the affair, but they were never paid. In spite of the fact that almost everyone who amounted to anything in Providence must have known the names of most of the sixty-four persons involved in the burning of the *Gaspée*, they kept their knowledge to themselves to the end of the war. Even a court of inquiry in 1773 discovered nothing.

The Rhode Island Historical Society's broadside which describes the episode of the burning of the *Gaspée* is entitled "A New Song, Called the Gaspée," and it is believed to have been written by Captain Swan of Bristol, who allegedly took part in the affair.

A New Song, Called the Gaspée

'Twas in the reign of George the Third,
Our public peace was much disturb'd
By ships of war, that came and laid
Within our ports, to stop the trade.

Sometimes they'd weigh and give them chase;
Such actions sure was very base;
No honest coasters cou'd pass by,
But what they would let some shot fly;

And did provoke to high degree,
Those true born sons of liberty;
So that they cou'd no longer bear
Those sons of Belial staying there,

But 'twas not long 'fore it fell out,
That William Duddingston, so stout,
Commander of the Gaspée tender,
Which he has reason to remember;

Because as people do assert,
He almost had his just desert
Here on the tenth day of last June,
Betwixt the hours of twelve and one.

Did chace the slope call'd the Hannah,
Of whom one Lindsey was commander;
They dog'd her up Providence sound,
And there the rascal got aground.

The news of it flew that very day
That they on Namquit Point did lay:
That night about half after ten,
Some Narragansett Indianmen,

Being sixty-four if I can remember,
Which made this stout coxcomb surrender;
And what was left of all their tricks
They in his britch a ball did fix,

Then set the men upon the land,
And burnt her up we understand;
Which thing provokes the King so high,
He said those men shall surely die.

So if he could but find them out,
The hangman he'll employ no doubt;
For he's declared in his passion,
He'll have them tried, a new fashion.

Now for to find these people out,
King George has offer'd very stout;
One thousand pounds to find out one
That wounded William Duddingston.

One thousand more he says he'll spare
For those who say they sheriffs were:
One thousand more there doth remain,
For to find out the leaders name.

Likewise five hundred pound per man
Of any one of all the clan,
But let him try his utmost skill,
I'm apt to think he never will
Find out any of those hearts of gold,
Though he should offer fifty fold.

27

A NEWPORT PIRATE

RICHARD TEW, hailing from Mardford, England, settled at Newport, Rhode Island, in 1640. Becoming a deputy there, he soon was well-known and highly respected. Fifty-one years later his adventuresome young grandson, Thomas, sailed into Bermuda, anxious to acquire a share in the sloop *Amity*, a vessel owned by prominent residents there.

He succeeded in getting himself appointed captain of the craft and obtaining a privateering commission, he enlisted a crew and departed from Bermuda.

Once out on the high seas Tew suggested to his men that they turn pirates. They agreed, shouting, "A gold chain or a wooden leg—we'll stand by you."

Tew soon captured a rich prize with fabulous treasures aboard. It was an Arabian vessel, and when the booty had been divided each member of the crew received three thousand pounds as his share.

After a visit to Madagascar, the *Amity* sailed toward

America, by chance meeting another pirate vessel under
the command of the infamous Captain Mission. Mission,
who had established a pirate Utopia at Madagascar called
Libertatia, invited Tew for a visit there. The Rhode Islander enjoyed what he discovered at Libertatia and lived
for some time at the pirate kingdom. Finally he sailed out
on a mission to capture slaving vessels. Freeing the slaves,
he brought them back to Libertatia where they were
given equal privileges with the pirates. Tew and Mission
claimed that they wished to build up a strong, faithful
island empire free from class distinctions.

The Newport pirate's next venture was to chart and
survey the treacherous Madagascar coast, a task which
took four months. Although he did an excellent job, not
a single copy of his chart exists today.

Thomas then decided to establish a trade route between
Newport, Rhode Island, and the pirate kingdom. He was
already a very prosperous man when he sailed away from
Libertatia. He set his course first for the island of Bermuda, but a bad gale which sprung his mast forced him
off the course. After beating about for two weeks he
decided to head directly for his Newport home, which he
reached a week later. Despite his lawless occupation
he was received with much respect on arriving ashore,
especially when it was found out how wealthy he had
become.

Waiting to hear from him in Bermuda, however, were
the five co-owners of the *Amity*. Included in their members was one of the governor's council! Tew at once sent
a dispatch to them, asking for an agent to come to Newport to receive their shares of the vessel's trip. When
Captain Starrs, the representative appointed by the Bermuda partners, sailed into Newport Harbor, he discovered

that some of the money had been buried by Thomas, while the rest was deposited in Boston. The total amount constituted substantial profits for all concerned. Governor's Councilman William Outerbridge became richer by over three thousand pounds, receiving his share in "Lyon dollars and Arabian gold." Tew, himself, was able to bank around eight thousand pounds for his efforts on the high seas. He brought so many Arabian gold pieces into Newport that for a time these sizable coins, worth twice the value of Spanish dollars, were common not only there but in New York as well!

The captain journeyed to Boston to apply for a new privateering commission, but the cautious commissioners refused his request. Undaunted, Tew easily persuaded them to change their minds with a bribe of five hundred pounds. Armed now with this authority to capture French ships, Thomas went to New York where he located one Frederick Phillips, of whom he had heard. Phillips, known as one of the "brethren," at once declared himself interested in Tew's contemplated voyage to Madagascar. The ship *Frederick* was outfitted and made ready for sea, and a few weeks later Tew sailed with a full cargo for the port of Libertatia. After a relatively uneventful journey he reached the Madagascar coast.

Pleased with Tew's success, Captain Mission welcomed him heartily, and the rich cargo of New England merchandise was brought ashore and distributed. After a few weeks had gone by, Mission suggested to Tew that a cruise to the Red Sea might prove lucrative to both of them. For this purpose Mission furnished two large ships, each manned by two hundred and fifty men, and the voyage began.

Off the Arabian coast the two captains fell in with a

ship of the Great Mogul, packed with sixteen hundred
pilgrims on the way to Mecca. Although the Great
Mogul's vessel carried more than one hundred guns, there
was no real force to man them, and when the pirates
sailed into battle against them the pilgrims offered little
effective resistance. Boarding the ship, the pirates cut
their way through the passengers, and the encounter
was soon over. Not one of the buccaneers was killed, and
they promptly started a systematic examination of their
prize. After stripping the vessel of all treasure, they decided to consider taking some of the females on board
back to their island stronghold. It seems that the lack
of suitable women at the pirate Shangri-La was one of
the few things which caused discontent among the men.
After declaring their marital status, the unmarried girls
were placed in one part of the ship while the wives were
congregated elsewhere. About one hundred single girls
between twelve and eighteen years of age could be accommodated without trouble back in Libertatia, and despite the entreaties of the Mecca-bound Mohammedans,
the captive maidens were removed to the pirate vessels.

The return journey to Libertatia began with the pilgrim
ship in company. As the Great Mogul's craft was a poor
sailor, she was taken apart. She had yielded countless
treasures in diamonds, silks and gold, and her hundred
guns were mounted in two batteries near the harbor's
mouth. Except for the hapless unmarried girls, the survivors of the capture were allowed to return home as best
they could.

Affairs were now progressing in such a favorable manner that certain features of the pirate colony resembled
a glorified Brook Farm project. The prosperous settlement was by this time strongly fortified, and a farming

community was being developed in the rear of the village where several scores of acres of land were being cultivated. Three hundred head of sturdy black cattle grazed on the rolling fields nearby, and a great commercial pier was completed. Each pirate had chosen his own location for a home, which accommodated not one but two, three or four of the wives of his particular choice.

One beautiful morning some months after Thomas Tew had returned from America, one of the pirate sloops came sailing into the harbor chased by no less than five great ships of the Portuguese navy. It was a dangerous moment, but the pirates were equal to the occasion. Every cannon around the entire harbor system of fortifications was manned within a few minutes, and when the pursuers drew abeam of the fort, Tew was in command of all the English-speaking pirates on the island while Mission had charge of the other nationalities.

All but one of the five Portuguese warships successfully ran past the outer system of fortifications, but when they reached the inner harbor they received such a merciless pounding that two of the attackers were immediately sunk. Devastating fire was poured into the remaining vessels by the combined efforts of the shore batteries and the pirate ships in the harbor. A third vessel was boarded and taken, while the captains of the two Portuguese men-of-war still afloat, realizing that the battle was lost, ran for the harbor's entrance to escape. They made it successfully, although they were badly damaged, and sailed away. It is said that this engagement became the subject of pirate conversation all over the world for years to come. A pirate stronghold on the Madagascar coast had defeated a fleet of the best ships of the Portuguese navy!

The Newport pirate had acquitted himself well in the

fight. As a reward, Tew was now made Admiral of the
Fleet. With this new honor he began to have great
dreams of a powerful piratical empire. He suggested a
voyage to the Indian Sea to gather new recruits. The
colony, he thought, was rich enough, but needed fresh
blood. Leaving Libertatia on board the flagship *Victorie,*
with three hundred of the most hardened pirates manning
his guns and yards, Tew decided to call on his old quar-
termaster who had left the *Amity* to settle ashore on
another part of the island of Madagascar. The quarter-
master, now governor of the area, was pleased to see his
former captain again, but declined, as did the others in
his colony, to leave their idyllic settlement. They were
living in comfort and security with plenty of their treasure
still intact, and the governor had no wish to go to sea
again. But he asked the Rhode Islander to stay for the
afternoon and had a feast prepared for the occasion. At
the height of the banquet, however, a storm arose to
churn the waters into a frightful gale, throwing the *Victorie* ashore on a rugged, dangerous promontory near the
settlement. All of the pirates aboard were drowned in
full sight of their captain, who could give them no assistance.

This sudden change in the fortunes of the Newport
pirate crew came as a great shock to Tew, who not only
was left without a ship but had no means of communicat-
ing with the home port. Back at Libertatia, when weeks
passed without word from the buccaneer, Captain Mission
started a search for him. Two sloops sailed into the quar-
termaster's harbor some weeks later, to the Rhode Islander's great happiness. His joy was short-lived, however, for
Captain Mission had tragic news of his own. After Tew's
departure, another pirate vessel, the *Bijoux,* had also left

the settlement with a large force of buccaneers aboard. Probably through the offices of a spy, it became known to the natives that the pirate stronghold had been seriously weakened by the absence of the two ships. Seizing the opportunity, they secretly prepared to attack Libertatia.

Tew was told that the invasion of the colony had started in the dead of night. As the natives stormed the settlement, men, women and children were slaughtered without mercy. The weakened garrison proved no match for the determined Madagascars, who had old scores to settle. Captain Mission, seeing the way the battle was going, fled to the waterfront, where he boarded a sloop. Hoisting sail, he and a small group hastily left the harbor. Another sloop later got away, but only forty-five pirates survived the onslaught. In spite of his hasty exit, Mission departed with a substantial amount of diamonds and gold.

After the pirate captains had commiserated with each other, the Newport pirate proposed a new journey to America where they could settle unmolested in either Newport or New York. But Mission claimed that he was homesick for his family in France and would have to return to the Continent before deciding. He gave Tew one of the sloops, however, and divided his diamonds and gold. The two parted company, Mission sailing away with a crew of fifteen, while Tew set out from Madagascar with thirty-four Englishmen.

More trouble lay ahead, however. Running into a violent storm on the way to the Cape of Good Hope, Captain Mission's sloop went down within a short distance of Tew's vessel, and the Newport pirate was unable to save his friend. It was such a terrific storm that not a single pirate could be saved from the raging seas.

The rest of the journey around the Cape of Good Hope
and across the Atlantic to America was more or less uneventful, with the sloop arriving safely in Newport Harbor
a few weeks later. Here Tew divided his treasure with
the members of his crew who, it has been said, hied off
to Boston, where they "shewed themselves publicly," on
the streets of that sedate city.

The captain, however, settled down quietly at Newport, where he lived in peace. Gradually others of his
crew returned to Newport, one of them, Thomas Jones,
marrying Penelope Goulden and remaining in Rhode Island.

The governor of New York, Benjamin Fletcher, was a
good friend of Thomas Tew, and could often be seen
with the notorious pirate on the streets of New York, nor
did he mind dining him at his palatial home. Of course,
Tew had many dealings in New York, where he disposed
of a large share of his uncut diamonds. Governor Fletcher,
like some other colonial governors, was always ready to
turn "an honest penny." And so it was that when Tew
presented himself at the governor's mansion on November
4, 1694, to apply for a privateering commission to go on
a voyage which his crew had urged, Fletcher readily con-
sented—for the payment of three hundred pounds.

A few days later the Rhode Island captain sailed from
Newport Harbor aboard the *Amity*. He was joined shortly
by two other vessels, one a sloop commanded by Captain
Wake, an old pirate pardoned by King James, and the
other a brigantine captained by Master Want, Tew's mate
on his first trip. Others who made the voyage included
Thomas Jones of Newport who left his Penelope at the
pier. Tew's fleet was further augmented by the appearance of Captain Glover in a ship from New York. By

June, 1695, the fleet had reached Liparau Island at the mouth of the Red Sea, where Tew joined the pirate armada of the great and equally famous "Long Ben" Avery.*

A week later twenty-five Arab ships passed their fleet in the dead of night. When Avery heard the news, he started in quick pursuit. The *Amity*, unfortunately, could not match the fast pace which its companion set and so fell behind. Meanwhile, Avery soon came up with a Moorish ship, from which he took sixty thousand pounds in gold and silver. Then another craft was sighted, overhauled and captured, this time with one hundred and eighty thousand pounds to be divided.

It is not known whether or not Captain Tew ever heard of the rich treasure taken from these Moorish ships, but he fell in with another one of the fleet some days later and attacked it. Perhaps his luck had turned or their easygoing life had softened both him and the crew. In any case, when the Moors offered unexpected resistance to the Yankee pirate, Tew realized that he was face to face with defeat that afternoon. Suddenly a shot carried away a portion of his stomach, and in the words of Captain Johnson, Tew "held his Bowels with his Hands some small Space; when he dropp'd, it struck such a Terror in his men, that they suffered themselves to be taken, without making Resistance."

And so pirate Thomas Tew died, far from his native Newport, where he had planned to live in peace and comfort during his declining years. I often wonder what happened to the contents of one chest that he left behind, mentioned in the *Calendar of State Papers* for 1696 and

---

* See my *True Tales of Pirates and Their Gold,* pages 56-67.

1697. It was so heavy "that six men at the tackles" could hardly hoist it. Several descendants of Tom Tew live today not far from Newport, whence their ancestor sailed to plunder the seas in the year 1691.

28

LABDEN'S LEAP

A MARINER SAILING INTO the general vicinity of Long Island Sound about twenty-five miles east of New York would find himself to the south of Greenwich, Connecticut, and to the north of the Oyster Bay region of Long Island. Should he desire to explore the Connecticut coastline and steer north, he could go ashore in Greenwich. After suitable inquiries, he would be told the approximate location of the famed Labden's Leap Rock, about halfway between the railroad and the Post Road, not far from the location where the Myanos River enters Long Island Sound.

Early in the seventeenth century a blockhouse was built in the dense forest at the location where the river meets the sound, and our legend begins there one September day in the year 1645. Two middle-aged men, Captain Daniel Patrick and Captain John Underhill, were striding along outside the blockhouse. Broadswords dangled from their cross belts, and massive pistols were thrust through their girdles. They seemed well able to handle almost any situation which might arise, but it was evident that they were extremely worried.

Captain Patrick was the leader of the relatively small colony which had set up a village here. Having chafed under Puritan laws elsewhere, Patrick had led a small group of free-thinking English settlers to the Myanos River.

These pioneers had been joined by a few Dutch immigrants from New Amsterdam, among them a bold hunter and trapper named Cornelius Labden. Unlike the other colonists who for the most part were farmers, Labden made his living in the fur trade. As soon as he had amassed a fine collection of pelts, he was accustomed to ride by horseback to the Dutch trading post known as Byram Fort, just over the line which now separates the states of New York and Connecticut. After selling his pelts, the trader would return to his home, a remarkable log cabin built near the edge of a towering precipice. He had chosen for his abode the very top of this rocky cliff, more than one hundred feet high, which was located at least two miles from the outskirts of the settlement. Cornelius had married an English girl, and they had been blessed with two fine children, Hans and Anneke.

On the day that Patrick and Underhill were discussing the possible danger of attack by the Indians, Cornelius rode up to the blockhouse with the load of pelts he was taking to the trading post.

"Greeting, Cornelius!" shouted Patrick. "We are talking about whether or not the Indians plan to remain peaceful. What do you think about it?"

"I am afraid we will have trouble," answered Cornelius. "The other day Chief Owenoke said to me, 'Cornelius,

Indian's friend, had better go away.' Yes, Owenoke's father Ponus means trouble as soon as the snow flies."

"Well, if that is your belief don't leave with your pelts for Byram Fort until I finish a letter to Governor Kieft. I'll write it at once," said Patrick.

Within an hour Patrick had penned an appeal to the Dutch to have a company of musketeers sent to the trading post at Byram, as Patrick expected the entire region soon to be ravaged "for many miles with torch and tomahawk." The letter was addressed to Wilhelm Kieft, Governor General of New Netherlands at New Amsterdam. Patrick impressed Labden with the importance of telling the authorities at Byram Fort that the letter should be sent with great speed.

Patrick did not feel as Cornelius Labden did, that the Indians would wait for a fall of snow, but believed the red men might strike at any moment. Although the people were busy gathering their crops, Patrick soon made it a practice to have all women and children in the immediate vicinity brought into the blockhouse every night. He neglected, however, to care for Labden's family, as they were too far away from the settlement. Probably the Indians observed every move which the white people made, and when they saw the women and children withdrawn into the blockhouse at nightfall, they decided that they might as well strike at once.

Three days after Labden left for Byram the attack came. The colonists were all working in the fields, and the men kept their muskets close at hand. Suddenly the dreaded war whoops sounded across the valley. The brave farmers met the savage onslaught, the men quickly loading and firing their weapons as their families started running toward the blockhouse. The settlers covered the retreat of the women and children, firing repeatedly, but Indian arrows killed at least three of them before they could reach protection.

Once in the shelter of the compound, the colonists were organized into two groups of fighting men, Patrick leading one platoon and Underhill the other. At a given signal the great doors of the stockade swung open. The platoons poured out, charging the savages fiercely on either flank and driving them back with heavy losses.

The red men now began the systematic burning of all log cabins in the area. Cornelius Labden's home was soon in flames and his wife and children taken into captivity. The Indians, however, did not leave the vicinity after their destruction of the homes as the colonists had hoped, and they soon began a siege of the blockhouse.

Three days later, early in the morning, the English settlers were aroused by the hoofbeats of a galloping horse. It was Cornelius Labden, returning from the west along the bank of the Myanos River. The Indians had destroyed the log bridge which led over the river, but Labden urged his beast to jump into the water and swim across. Arrows struck in the stream all around him, several stinging both horse and rider.

Hearing the noise, Captain Underhill led a score of colonists out from the palisades and opened up a heavy fire on the Indians lining the banks of the river. Under cover of this protection, Labden landed safely on the eastern bank of the Myanos and reported to Captain Underhill. Because of the urgency of the letter entrusted to him, he had been ordered to go all the way to New Amsterdam with the message instead of leaving it a Byram Fort, and he brought back the heartening new that even then a Dutch company of musketeers was marching to help.

The women and children from the stockade now came trooping out of the blockhouse to get the news, but Cornelius looked in vain for his own family.

"My God," he cried in anguish. "Did you forget my own wife and children while I delivered your letter? Is that your idea of fair play?"

"It wasn't like that at all," answered Patrick. "You yourself said that the Indians would not attack until a wintry snowstorm had struck, but they came unexpectedly while we were out in the cornfields."

"You do not explain how all these other women and children were saved at the time, then, do you?" replied the heartbroken Cornelius, and retired alone in his grief to a corner of the stockade.

A little later Patrick walked up to him.

"Cornelius, do not blame us. We only took in the women and children of those who lived within easy distance, and there were others who lived not more than a mile away who were not saved. Your family lived two miles distant."

"Patrick," replied Cornelius Labden, "it is true there may have been others lost, but they did not have their man carrying messages to New Amsterdam for you. No matter how you look at it, you have been negligent."

"Cornelius, listen to me. Your Indian friends were among those who took your wife and children after they burned your cabin. Chief Owenoke would never kill your family, for you are Dutch, and not English. Probably your wife and children are living captive."

But the shocking blow of his family's uncertain fate was too much for Labden. Muttering to himself in

Dutch, he began to dart wild looks around the stockade. Suddenly he sprang to his feet.

"Open the gate," he bellowed in a commanding and fearsome tone. Although a few attempted to seize his horse's head and prevent Cornelius from leaving, several of the men were so overwhelmed by his manner that they swung the great stockade door open, and the rider thundered outside the enclosure on his sturdy beast.

As the sound of hoofbeats grew feebler, Patrick and the others wondered what would happen to the grief-maddened trapper. Meanwhile, Labden was riding as fast as his horse could carry him for his ruined log cabin two miles away. As he passed first one and then another of the ravaged homesteads, he grew angrier and angrier at his former friends, the Indians.

Galloping along near an Indian camp, his mad shouts attracted the attention of half a dozen braves, who leaped to their mounts and started to ride after him. Reaching an open plateau, he turned in his saddle, aimed his gun and fired with accuracy. He was gratified to see one of the six Indians drop off his horse to his death, but the five surviving red men kept up their pursuit.

Labden now developed a plan. Slowing his horse's speed gradually, he allowed the remaining Indians to gain ground until they were directly behind him. He was on the trail which led high up the hillside to his cabin on the rocky cliff, from which there could be no turning back. As he neared the end of the trail where he could see the still-smoldering remains of his cabin he headed for the trees concealing the steep precipice below.

At the very moment when he was about to enter the grove, a tomahawk whizzed through the air and struck him violently in the shoulder, but he did not slacken his pace. When he reached the first of the trees, he twisted slightly in his saddle, and seemed to dare the red men to follow him. Then he continued on the remaining stretch to the ledge at a gallop and barely hesitating, leaped into space. Immediately, the shrieks of the pursuing Indians rent the air as they followed into Labden's trap.

The first four red men hurtled down through the air in their final fleeting seconds of life, realizing, too late, how they had been tricked. The very last Indian, having witnessed the predicament of his comrades, was able to scramble off his steed at the last moment. Slithering down the face of the cliff, he crashed into a tree fifty feet below, where he clung desperately for a moment, and then recovered himself. His companions and their mounts were killed almost instantly.

Cornelius, on the other hand, knew the cliff intimately, and at the last second urged his horse far to the left where he could expect to land on softer ground. Although his animal was fatally injured in the hundred-foot drop, the trapper survived.

The remaining Indian, who had managed to climb up the cliff, limped back to his tribe and told them the fantastic story of the leap of death, a tale which was repeated for many years by their descendants.

The very night of Labden's ruse, the Dutch soldiers from New Amsterdam arrived at the blockhouse. In a battle fought soon afterward they met and defeated the Indians, driving them far to the north. They found Cornelius the following morning still alive but battered, with many of his bones broken. Moreover, his mind was affected by the entire experience, and he became merely a shell of his former vigorous self.

Two years later the combined forces of Dutch and

English troops stormed the Sinoway village of the Indians who had been the leaders in the Myanos River massacre. After this action the settlers returned and re-established their shattered homes.

Ten years passed. Pleasant farms and estates had sprung up around the Myanos River, and on one of them, the residence of Captain Underhill, Cornelius Labden lived, now a hopeless cripple. He spent most of his time smoking his long Dutch pipe and looking out over Long Island Sound, as if he almost expected his lost family might be brought back to him from that direction. He had been told of the discovery of his wife's body a few miles from the ruins of his log cabin but he hoped that some day he would hear from his children.

One fine summer afternoon he was sitting in his usual place on Captain Underhill's porch, mumbling to himself. It was a perfect day, and the view of the sound was an inspiring one. Suddenly, an Indian youth walked over to the side of the building and stood in the grass looking up at the crippled trapper.

Noticing the visitor, Labden closed his eyes as if to shut out what he had seen. Then he opened them and waved the boy away. But the redskin did not move, and Cornelius now regarded him carefully for the first time. He had blue eyes and brown hair, which did not seem to go with the copper skin, the breech clout and the moccasins. Noticing that the old man was now glaring at him intently, the Indian spoke.

"Me find Lapten, me find Lapten," he said. The young brave's manner was sincere, and the sound of his voice apparently awakened long-forgotten memories in the mind of the shattered being who had once been a fearless hunter. Instinctively he answered the boy in the Dutch language, and the youth listened earnestly, seeming to recognize certain of the words.

As Cornelius noticed the effect his speech had on the Indian, he began to tremble. For the first time in many years his eyes were now burning with intelligence and interest.

At that moment the venerable Captain Underhill entered the kitchen. Labden stood up, alert, and his very manner showed that a great change had come over him.

"Come," he said to the boy, and led him into the house. Reaching the kitchen, Cornelius pumped water up from the well into a pan. Then he began to wash the young Indian's face, and in a few moments clear white skin appeared from under the paint.

"Captain, Captain Underhill! My Hans has come back to me. Hans, tell me where is Anneke?" In a burst of recognition, Cornelius threw his arms around his son's neck and began to sob passionately.

Hans told his father how he and Anneke had been carried off by savages into the northern regions of New England. The children had been separated, and Hans never saw his sister again.

As he grew older, Hans forgot much of his past, but he did retain the memory of his father's name and the fact that he was white. Finally he escaped from his adopted tribe. Working his way down to Connecticut again, he reached the Myanos River, where his query of "Me find Lapten" eventually sent him to Captain Underhill's home and his own father.

THE HOLOCAUST OF
LONG ISLAND SOUND

FOR WELL OVER A CENTURY the legend of the terrible fire aboard the side-wheeler *Lexington*, whenever it has been discussed, has caught the popular imagination of residents both in New York and New England. Unfortunately, in the telling and retelling of this awesome event people have allowed much which is pure fabrication to creep into the story.

Early in 1931, I was given the opportunity to acquire copies of the entire inquest proceedings, and later studied the holocaust from the point of view of recovering the treasure, a fabulous amount of bullion, which was believed to have gone down with the burning excursion craft. I had been definitely told that a substantial sum of money was still at the bottom of the Long Island Sound area where the *Lexington* finally sank. At one time, I was even interested in a very attractive skin-diving plan to search the scene of the disaster for the sunken wealth.

However, information now in my possession assures me that practically all the specie which was aboard the *Lexington* when she sailed that fateful day never even reached the bottom of the sea at all. Because of my knowledge that there is little if any treasure in Long Island Sound at the scene of the *Lexington's* sinking, I am now able to reveal, without betraying any confidence, the entire story of the *Lexington* disaster as it never could be told before.

On the afternoon of Monday, January 13, 1840, Captain George Child sailed the 205-foot excursion steamboat *Lexington* from her New York pier bound for Stonington, Connecticut. After backing out of the dock, the *Lexington* threaded her way up the East River through Hell Gate and into Long Island Sound. The final streaks of sunset were lost in the western sky by this time, and the boisterous January winds began to lash the afterdeck.

In various parts of the steamer there were coastwise travelers, merchants and round-the-world sea captains, discussing national and local affairs. A few tables for the card players had been set up, and those who enjoyed the games were busy at their chosen pastime. The returning sea captains gathered around one of the stoves to tell of their voyages and talk over their homecoming. Some of these master mariners had been away from their loved ones for several years and were happy with the thoughts of the coming family reunions.

At seven-thirty that night the *Lexington* was proceeding off Eaton's Neck, Long Island. Suddenly a single cry full of alarm and terror was heard echoing through the steamer. *"Fire,"* came the shout, which was picked up and repeated everywhere. Soon the passengers all knew the fearsome news. The worst marine calamity possible, a fire at sea, had broken out. A vessel may weather a thousand storms, but disaster is inevitable aboard a burning ship unless the fire is brought under immediate control.

Second Mate David Crowley rushed to the scene of the blaze near the smokestack, and quickly organized a fire-bucket brigade. Pail after pail of water was thrown in vain on the growing flames, which by now had assumed terrifying proportions. The vital minutes passed, and the men fought on until their burned and blackened bodies could stand no more. As the blaze forced its relentless way ahead, Captain Child finally told the bucket brigade to drop back, for the *Lexington* was doomed, and the steamer was now headed for the nearest shore.

Across Long Island Sound at Southport, Connecticut, Captain Meeker of the sloop *Merchant* watched the burning boat steaming up the coast. Attempting to sail his sloop to the rescue, he ran her aground on the outer bar. It was not until several hours later when the tide turned, that Meeker was able to arrive at the scene to render assistance, but by that time few passengers were alive to help.

Another small boat put out from the Long Island shore, but the speed of the *Lexington* was so great and the water was so rough that the smaller craft gave up and returned to port.

Finally the captain of the *Lexington* realized that he would have to abandon ship. In a calm voice he cried out, "Gentlemen, take to the boats." This started a rush for the lifeboats while the steamer was still making too much headway for the launching of a small craft into the choppy seas. Regardless of this danger, the panic-stricken passengers put over a lifeboat from the forward part of the steamer. The small boat, caught in the waves, was swamped instantly. If the passengers had waited until the engine stopped they would have had more chance of launching it successfully.

I can do no better at this time than to quote from the sworn testimony presented at the inquest into the *Lexington* disaster. A passenger, Captain Hillard, made the following statement at the proceedings held ten days after the terrible event in Long Island Sound:

"I am 24 years of age. I reside at Port Ann, New York. I went aboard a week ago last Monday, the 13th, about 3 P.M. to go to Stonington. I was bound to Norwich.

"It was about an hour after supper that I first heard the alarm of fire. I was then on the point of turning in, and had my coat and boots off. I slipped them on. I then discovered the casing of the smoke pipe, and I think, a part of the promenade deck, on fire. There was a great rush of the passengers and much confusion, so that I could not notice particularly. The after part of the casing was burning, and the fire was making aft. I thought at the time that the fire might be subdued; but being aft at the time, could not, therefore see distinctly.

"I shortly after went on the promenade deck; my attention had previously been directed to the passengers, who were rushing into the quarter boats; and when I went on the quarter deck, the boats were both filled. They seemed to be stupidly determined to destroy themselves, as well as the boats, which were their only means of safety. I went to the starboard boat, which they were lowering away; they lowered it until she took the water, and then I saw someone cut away the forward tackle fall;

it was at all events disengaged, and no one at the time could have unhooked the fall; the boat instantly filled with water, there being at the time about twenty persons in her; and the boat passed immediately astern, entirely clear.

"I then went to the other side; the other boat was cleared away and lowered in the same manner as the first, full of passengers. This boat fell astern entirely disengaged, as the other had done, but fell away before she had entirely filled with water.

"By this time the fire had got under such headway, that I pretty much made my mind up 'it was a gone case.' The fire by this time began to come up around the promenade deck, and the wheel-house was completely filled with smoke. There were two or three on the promenade deck near the wheel-house, and their attention was turned to the life boat; it was cleared away.

"I assisted in stripping off the canvas, but I had no notion of going in her, as I had made my mind up that they would serve her as they had done the other boats . . . The smoke was so dense that I could not see distinctly what they were about. I think that the communication with the fore part of the boat was by this time cut off; from the first hearing of the alarm, perhaps twenty minutes had elapsed. The engine had now been stopped about five minutes. I recommended to the few deck hands and passengers who remained, to throw the cotton overboard; and told them they must do something for themselves, and the best thing they could do was to take the cotton. There were perhaps ten or a dozen bales thrown overboard which was pretty much all there was on the larboard side which had not taken fire.

"I then cut off a piece of line, perhaps four or five

fathoms, and with it spanned a bale of cotton, which, I believe, was the last one not on fire. It was a very snug, square bale, about four feet long and three feet wide, and a foot and a half thick. Aided by one of the firemen, I put the bale up on the rail, round which we took a turn, slipped the bale down below the guard, when we both got on to it. The boat then lay broadside to the wind, and we were under the lee of the boat, on the larboard side. We placed ourselves one on each end of the bale, facing each other; with our weight it was about one-third out of the water. The wind was pretty fresh, and we drifted at the rate of about a knot and a half."

Captain Hillard and his fellow survivor, Benjamin Cox decided not to lash themselves to the bale but coiled the rope up in the middle. They then pushed away from the burning craft, as it was getting unbearably hot. Shoving the bale around to the stern, they finally left the burning *Lexington* around eight o'clock that night. Captain Hillard found a stick in the water, which he used for a paddle. In this manner he kept the bale facing into the sea.

When the two men pushed away from the ship, there were few living persons still aboard the *Lexington*. Most of them had either perished in the swamping of the boats, or had jumped into the water. As the men sat astride their bale of cotton, the waves sloshed against their bodies until they were wet up to the waist. Every half hour Hillard glanced at his watch. The wreck did not sink until three o'clock the next morning. It was then so cold that the men kept up their circulation by violently beating their arms against their wet bodies. An hour later, the great bale rolled over. Clambering up on top of the other side, the men could not find their paddle and conditions rapidly became worse.

Cox soon lost courage at the turn events had taken and lapsed into a coma. Hillard tried to revive him, but in vain. Suddenly the bale gave a quick lurch. Cox rolled off into the water and failed to come up. That was the last Captain Hillard ever saw of him.

Back in Southport, Captain Meeker had finally got his sloop off the bar. Sailing in the direction which the *Lexington* had taken, he came upon Captain Hillard lying across the bale of cotton. Hillard was carried aboard the sloop, where he was given every possible attention. A short time later Captain Meeker fell in with two other survivors, one on another bale of cotton, and the second floating with the help of a section of the guard rail. They were quickly revived and were able to tell their stories.

The two men who had been taken from the water at this time were Captain Stephen Manchester, pilot of the *Lexington*, and Charles Smith, a deckhand.

The pilot of the *Lexington*, who was rescued by Captain Meeker, gave important testimony which was sworn to at the inquest. Captain Manchester's statements follow:

"When I first heard the alarm of fire, about half past seven o'clock, some one came to the wheel-house door and told me that the boat was on fire; my first movement was to step out of the wheel-house and look aft; saw the upper deck burning all round the smoke pipe, the flames coming up through the promenade deck. I returned into the wheel-house and put the wheel hard-a-port to steer the boat for the land. I then thought it very doubtful whether the fire could be extinguished.

"We were about four miles from Long Island shore, and at the rate we were then going, it would take about twenty minutes to reach it.

"We had not yet headed to the land, when something gave way, which I believe was the tiller rope; I think she was heading about south-east, and Long Island bore about south, when the tiller rope gave way; the engine was then working; and the boat fell ahead more to the eastward. Captain Child then came into the wheel-house and put his hand to the spoke of the wheel, and, as he did so, the rope gave way; I presume it was the rope attached to the wheel; it was the larboard rope gave way; and at the same time the smoke came into the wheel-house, and we were obliged to go out.

"I suspect he went aft, but I never saw him afterwards; when he went out he went down on the forward deck; I do not recollect whether he expressed any alarm. I then called to them on the forecastle to get out the fire engine and buckets; the engine was got out, but they could not get at the buckets, or at least I only saw a few. I am of opinion the wheel-ropes burnt off, but I could not have stood it longer even if there had been chains round the wheel. I think there was then an opportunity to go from the wheel-house aft, where there was another steering apparatus, a good tiller, with chains which ran through blocks; all boats are so rigged, in order that if anything happens to the rudder, this can be used in its place. I did not go aft to it, because I thought my services would be more useful forward.

"After calling to get out the engine, I went to the life boat, and found some persons taking the tarpaulin off it. I caught hold of the lashing of the boat, and requested them not to let her go until we got a line fastened to her. I called to those at the forecastle to pass a line to make fast to her, which they did, and we fastened it to her bow. The fire was then burning through the promenade deck. I cut the lashing, and told them to launch the boat. I jumped from the promenade deck down on the forward deck, took hold of the hawser, and found it was not fastened to the steamboat. I told them to hold on to the rope, but they all let go one after another; the engine was still going, and I was obliged to let it go myself also.

"We then found two buckets, and commenced throwing water with them and the specie boxes; we got the water from over the side of the boat, which was then nearly stopped; while doing this, some others took the flag-staffs and parts of the bulwarks, and made a raft, to which we made a line fast and hove it over the side of the boat; we then threw the baggage overboard from four baggage cars, and made them fast with a line; the engine by this time was entirely stopped; it worked from ten to fifteen minutes going gradually slower until it ceased. We threw out everything by which we thought any person could save themselves; and continued throwing on water in hopes that some relief might reach us.

"The main deck now fell in as far as the capstan, and the people had by this time got overboard, some of them drowned, and others hurried on to the baggage cars, the raft and other things. What was left of the main deck was now on fire, and got us cornered up in so small a space that we could do nothing more by throwing water.

"There were then only eight or ten persons astern on the steamboat, and about thirty on the forecastle. They were asking me what they should do, and I told them I saw no chance for any of us; that if we stayed there, we should be burned to death, and if we went overboard we should probably perish. Among those who were there, was Mr. Hoyt and Van Cott, another person named

Harnden, who had charge of the express line. I did not
know anyone else.

"I then took a piece of spun yarn and made it fast to my
coat, and also to the rail, and so eased myself down upon
the raft. There were two or three others on it already, and
my weight sank it. I held on to the rope until it came up
again—and when it did, I sprang up and caught a piece
of railing which was in the water, and from thence got on
a bale of cotton where there was a man sitting; found the
bale was made fast to the railing; I took out my knife and
cut it off.

"At the time I cut this rope, I saw some person, standing on the piece of railing, who asked me if there was
room for another; I made no answer, and he jumped, and
knocked off the man that was with me; and I hauled him
on again. I caught a piece of board which was floating
past, and shoved the bale clean off the raft; and used the
board to endeavor to get in shore at Crane Neck Point,
in which I could not succeed; but I used the board as long
as I could, for exercise.

"When I left the wreck, I looked at my watch, and it
was just 12 o'clock. I think the man who was on the bale
with me said his name was McKenna and lived at New
York; he spoke of his wife and children; how he had
kissed them the morning he left home, and said he feared
he should perish with the cold.—He died about 3 o'clock.

"After I had hauled him on the bale, I had encouraged
him, and told him to thrash his hands, which he did for
a spell, but soon pretty much gave up. When he died he
fell back on the bale, and the first sea that came washed
him off. My hands were then so frozen that I could
hardly use them at all; I was about three miles from the
wreck when she sunk; and the last thing I recollect, was

seeing the sloop, and raising my handkerchief between my fingers hoping they would see me. I was then sitting on the cotton, with my feet in the water. The bale did not seem to roll at all, although there were some heavy seas.

"I was taken off the cotton by Captain Meeker, and brought to Southport, where I received every possible attention.

"I knew Captain Child for ten or fifteen years. He and I were packet masters for several years, and since then he has commanded the steamboats *Providence* and *Narraganset;* he was a man of considerable decision of character, and had commanded a steamboat for four years.

"When he came to the wheel-house on the night of the fire, he appeared to be agitated, but there was too short time for me to remark much. I think the fire originated from the smokepipe; it was very red that night, and the cotton was most likely piled within two feet of the steam chimney. The boat was going about twelve knots, but the engine went gradually slower until it stopped, which was about twenty minutes after the first alarm."

Charles B. Smith, fireman on board the *Lexington,* testified as follows:

"The first time I heard the alarm of fire was about half past 7 o'clock in the evening. I was in my room asleep, on the guard; a man came in and told me that the boat was on fire; I got out of my berth; the door of the room was open, directly opposite the steam chimney, and I saw the promenade deck, and part of the casing around the chimney on fire; went immediately into the crank room and put on the hose, opened the cocks, and tried to get to the end of the hose to play on the fire, but the fire and smoke prevented me.

"The hose was lying alongside of the bulkhead, alongside of the air pump. I went aft of the shaft to get breath, and then tried to get the buckets down that hung over the shaft, which the fire prevented me from doing; I then went aft with the intention of getting into the boat; I there saw Captain Child standing on the rail, by the crane of the boat, on the starboard side, and heard him sing out for the engineer; the engineer answered; and the captain asked him if he could stop the engine; he replied that it was impossible, as the fire prevented; I had now got to where Captain Child stood, and saw the bow tackle of the boat cut away, with the boat full of passengers—the bow of the boat filled with water, and she swung round on her stern tackle.

"Captain Child sung out to hold on to the boat, and slipped down to the fender, outside of the bulwark. I slipped over after him; he stepped into the stern sheets of the boat, and I put my foot on the stern of the boat, and hauled it back, and just as I got my foot back, the stern tackle was let go, but whether it was cut or not, I do not know. That was the last I saw of the boat or the Captain. Captain Child was in the boat at the time. I got over the stern then with the intention of getting on to the rudder; I hung by the netting, kicked in three cabin windows, and lowering myself down got on the rudder.

"I had been there but a minute or two, when I was followed by several others. There was a boy got over the stern, whom I told to drop overboard and get on a bale of cotton: he said he could not swim. I then told him to tell some of those on deck to throw over a bale of cotton. There was one thrown over, which I jumped on after, and gave the boy my place. I swam to it, and got on it. I remained on it until about half past 1 o'clock.

"About that time I drifted back to the steamboat and

got on board. There were then ten or twelve persons hanging to different parts of the boat. Mr. Hempstead was one of them, and one of the firemen by the name of Baum,—Job Sands, a waiter,—Harry Reed, and a small English boy,—another coal heaver, whose name was William, and a deck hand by the name of Charles. These were all the names I knew; the rest were, as I suppose, passengers, and some waiters,—there were no ladies. I staid there until 3 o'clock, when the boat sunk. I staid about midships, near where the fire originated.

"We stood on the top of the hips which are put on the boat to keep her from rolling, and are made of solid timber, running fore and aft of the boat nearly her whole length, under the guards; but the guards at this time were burnt off. I stood there until she sunk. After she began to fill, the rest jumped off.

"I then swam to a piece of the guard, and, with four others got on it,—they all perished before daylight. One of them was Harry Reed, and another, George, the fireman, the other was the boy to whom I had given my place on the rudder—the other I did not know; I think they all perished with the cold. I shook them all round, and tried to exercise them and rub them. I remained on the piece of guard until 2 o'clock in the afternoon, when I was taken off by the sloop *Merchant*, Captain Meeker, and was taken into Southport, where I had the best care taken of me possible. My feet were badly frozen, and my fingers touched a little with the frost.

"I have been in the *Lexington* ever since she commenced burning coal; knew her to be on fire on the 2nd of January, on the main deck, alongside the boiler; it originated from some sparks which flew up and caught the deck; it did not burn so much as to make a blaze on deck;

it burnt a corner of a box which was there, but did not damage the goods that were in it; never knew her on fire at any other time. When the door of the furnace is opened, the sparks from the coal do not come out unless the damper is down, which we always keep open and fastened open; I never saw the blaze come out of the furnace except when the damper was down.

"I never before saw the casing of the steam chimney on fire; I have seen the chimney red hot, and a blue flame come from the top of it, probably as much as six feet. I do not consider a boat in any more danger with a blower than without one; and we can make more steam with blowers than without; when we are carrying ten or twelve inches of steam, take off the blower and the steam will run down so as to stop on her centre in a short time; I have seen the steam run down sixteen inches to an inch and a half in twenty minutes after the blower was taken off."

Captain Comstock, who was hired by the *Lexington's* company to recover what material he could from the sound, sailed around the scene of the disaster on the Friday following the holocaust. Excerpts from his testimony follow:

"At 3 o'clock on Friday, A.M., I went on board the *Statesman*; at day-break we started, and landed again at Old Field Point. It was at this time intensely cold, the thermometer varying from three to four degrees below zero. At the Point I now left six men to look out for luggage, as I had heard that a number of trunks and packages had come ashore in the neighborhood. During the night, the body of a child about four years old had drifted ashore.

"At 8 o'clock A.M., I left in the steamer for the eastward.

Every part of the bank was carefully explored as we progressed, and traced the shore around the bay. I left persons ashore at different points, and inquired at all the houses for information relative to property saved from the wreck. After running seven miles east, I learned that three bodies had been found. I had them sent to Old Field Point; I have learned that eighteen miles farther east, a man had got ashore alive.

"I then proceeded to explore the beach the entire distance of the eighteen miles, until I came to the place. During this distance we found numerous portions of the wreck, among which was one piece, on which was the entire word 'Lexington,' in letters two feet long.

"We learned that David Crowley, the second mate, had come ashore at 5 o'clock on Wednesday night. He stated to the people here that he had been forty-eight hours upon the bale of cotton, and had crawled several rods upon the beach through the ice, and after getting ashore, had walked three quarters of a mile to the nearest house. They said that his feet and legs were badly frozen. He was bare-headed, and in his shirt sleeves; and supposed himself to be the only one saved from the wreck.* I gave instructions to leave nothing undone to render his situation as comfortable as possible, and to procure for him all medical or other aid that might be necessary. They said he was in the best of hands, and that he was in want of nothing for his comfort.

"We then left on our return to Old Field Point, to take on board, and bring to New York, the bodies and property which were there; having left information at all the places where we had stopped, that a reward would be

---

* This does not agree with Crowley's own account.

given for any bodies discovered, and offering also a reward of five hundred dollars for the detection of any
persons committing depredations upon the bodies or property which might come ashore from the wreck. I was
authorized to do this by the company. I was compelled to
relinquish the expedition on account of the severity of
the weather, and of the sudden accumulation of ice, which
rendered further efforts useless.

"On returning to the light-house, we took on board all
the baggage which had been collected by the men in my
absence,—five bodies, and the life-boat, which latter was
found about two miles to the westward of the light-house,
with the coats therein."

The remarkable story of David Crowley, the second
mate is a classic tale of the sea. At the very moment when
the other three survivors were being safely put ashore at
the Southport wharf, Crowley was still afloat on a cotton
bale some miles away. He had actually seen the *Merchant* rescue two of the survivors, whereupon he had
tried to wave to the captain but could not get his attention. The *Merchant* sailed away and the course of the
bale brought Crowley to a point off Faulkland Island. As
the cold was beginning to affect him, he tied his waistcoat
around his head for warmth and stuffed his clothing with
cotton from the bale, which he had cut open on the side.

Crowley had hoped the bale would touch the island,
but the tide carried him out to sea again. As soon as the
wind and surf went down, he stretched out on the bale
and fell asleep from exhaustion. Why did he not freeze
to death he never could understand, but when he awoke
the morning sun was shining in his face. He was completely refreshed by his slumbers.

All that day Crowley drifted on, hoping and praying for

rescue. As darkness fell, the bale suddenly bumped ashore, and Crowley sat up to find himself on a beach at the foot of a high bank. Sliding off the bale, he managed to crawl to the top of the hill, where he saw light shining from a house in the distance.

Step by step he forced his weary body toward the beacon in the darkness, finally arriving at the door of the home. Crowley was admitted just as the son of Mr. Huntington, the occupant, finished telling the story of the *Lexington* disaster. It was said afterward that Crowley presented a weird appearance, with his waistcoat tied around his head, and his clothes bulging with the warmth-bringing cotton, while he stood explaining his adventure. Crowley was given immediate care and later recovered.* He had come ashore at New Gully, Long Island, eighteen miles east of Old Field Point, having floated almost fifty miles!

A point discussed at the inquest was the closeness of the sloop *Improvement* at the time the *Lexington* was burning. Less than five miles away when he saw the blazing ship, Captain William Tirrell of the *Improvement* made the tragic decision not to bother going out to the *Lexington*, as he thought the burning vessel probably had enough lifeboats! Without question, he could have saved at least fifty persons and probably many more.

At the conclusion of the inquest the coroner's jury censured the steamboat inspectors and the owners of the side-wheeler for the terrible loss of life. Out of the 163 people aboard only four survived. Part of the jury voted

---

* He kept the cotton bale for many years, and did not relinquish it until during the Civil War, when Crowley's bale was sold to be made into bandages for dressing the wounded on the field of battle. From that bale came the famous "Lexington Brand" cloth.

in favor of fully exonerating the pilot, Captain Manchester, as it was shown that he had nothing to do with the loading of the cargo which later caught fire. However, as he was the sole surviving officer of the *Lexington,* in the custom of the sea, he had to be the target of censure during the inquest.

Actually, another small boat did get away successfully from the burning *Lexington,* although the inquest ended before the story reached New York. On the night of the fire which destroyed the steamer four men, watching their chances, waited until the forward progress of the vessel had stopped. Two of them were brothers, William A. Greene, of Providence, and David Greene, of Philadelphia. The other men were H. C. Craig and Charles Bracket, both of New York. William A. Greene had been entrusted with a chest in which a large amount of money was being shipped from New York City to Stonington, Connecticut. It is said that the value ran to five figures. Placing the chest in the center of their boat, the four men pushed away from the *Lexington* and were not seen alive again.

We will never know if these four men were dead when their boat finally came ashore, but the extreme cold of the below-zero temperature and the flying spray in the sound soon froze their bodies. It was a full week after the disaster before their boat was discovered frozen in the ice in a little cove at Stony Brook, Long Island.

At first William A. Greene was reported still alive, but actually he and three others, Craig, Bracket and Greene's brother David, had been frozen to death in such a manner that they were encased together in a thick coating of ice in the boat. William Greene was found straddling the treasure box which, with its thousands of dollars inside, had been frozen into the bottom of the boat under his body.

After cutting the bodies out of the boat, and taking them with the treasure chest on his wagon to the local authorities, the man who discovered the boat and its unusual cargo received a reward of one thousand dollars. The boat itself had been embedded in the ice so firmly "that a pair of oxen were required to drag it out." Also discovered at the same time was a writing desk belonging to a Salem mariner, "Captain Kimball, with considerable money" in the desk.

All the expeditions of the last 116 years organized to find the "bullion on the boat at the time she was lost," haven't had the slightest chance of success, for the treasure didn't go down on the *Lexington* at all.

INDEX

255